THE FIRST BOOK THAT SHOWS WOMEN HOW TO BUILD STRENGTH FOR THE DEMANDS OF MODERN LIFE.

Even the most physically fit woman may still be functioning well below her physical potential. If you are like most women, you have trouble lifting, carrying and moving heavy objects; prying open stuck windows and food jars; and excelling in the many sports that require strength.

Now Kathryn Lance, author of RUNNING FOR HEALTH AND BEAUTY, shows you how to build the necessary strength, endurance and suppleness for all these activities *without* building a "truckdriver physique."

GETTING STRONG
It can help every woman realize her physical potential.

Bantam Books by Kathryn Lance

GETTING STRONG
RUNNING FOR HEALTH AND BEAUTY:
A Complete Guide for Women

GETTING STRONG

A WOMAN'S GUIDE TO REALIZING HER PHYSICAL POTENTIAL

BY KATHRYN LANCE

BANTAM BOOKS
TORONTO · NEW YORK · LONDON

GETTING STRONG: A WOMAN'S GUIDE TO REALIZING
HER PHYSICAL POTENTIAL
*A Bantam Book / published by arrangement with
The Bobbs-Merrill Company, Inc.*

PRINTING HISTORY
Bobbs-Merrill edition published February 1978
2nd printing ....*March 1978*
3rd printing ....*April 1978*
Bantam edition / March 1979

Illustrations by Betty de Araujo

Cover photograph by Harry Benson

This book is dedicated with love
to my parents,
John F. and Kathryn H. Lance

ACKNOWLEDGMENTS

This book would not have been possible without the invaluable advice of my consultants, Elliot Derfler, Associate Professor of Health and Physical Education, Hunter College of the City University of New York, and Dr. Raymond Welsh, Associate Professor, Department of Physical Education, Florida Atlantic University, Boca Raton, Florida. I want to thank them for their many excellent suggestions and comments as well as for their detailed reading of the manuscript for accuracy.

The studies on women's physical potential at the United States Military Academy at West Point provided the framework for my thoughts while I was preparing this book. I want to thank Dr. James A. Peterson, Associate Professor and Director of Upper Class Instruction, and Dr. Robert Stauffer, Director of Project Summertime, for taking time out from their busy schedules to discuss with me their experiences and findings during the first coed year at the Academy. My thanks also to Sunny Jones of West Point's Office of Information for her kind help and comments, and of course thanks to all the pioneering women cadets who made the West Point studies possible. Very special thanks to my good friends Captain Michael Kjolsrud, his wife Paula, and their children, Matthew, Christine, Alexander and Nicholas, for putting me up while I was conducting interviews at West Point and for sending me much valuable material.

I want to thank all the women who volunteered to be guinea pigs in my Basic Strength Program; even those who didn't stick with the program were extremely helpful. Though I don't have room to list everyone by name, I especially want to mention Elizabeth Baker, Bonnie Bryant, Louise Colligan, Carol Conn, Kathy Crisman, Jane Fliegel, Diane Hellriegel, Emily Isberg, Phyllis Keaton, Maryellen Kohn, Lois Markham, and Lynn Spaulding.

I am most grateful to my friends and colleagues at Scholastic Magazines for their help and understanding over the last months, especially Niel Glixon, Maury Kurtz, Richard Maynard, Carol Thielman, Jim Brownell, and Jovial Bob Stine. Thanks also to Bruce Weber and Herman L. Masin of *Scholastic Coach* for allowing me access to their extensive library.

Very special thanks to my editor, Diane Giddis, who is everything an editor should be: intelligent, conscientious, thorough, and encouraging.

Thanks to the following neighborhood people who helped me in many ways, tangible and spiritual: Bill Cothran from V za V, Joe Ambrosino and Alan Harbater from Naseralishah Book Shop, Steven Kessler and Stanley Sterenberg from the Athlete's Foot, Mike Roberts and Chris Humphrey from the All State Cafe, and everyone at the People's Copy Center. Finally, warm thanks to my friends and acquaintances not only for their support, but for keeping their snickers to a minimum while I "pumped tomato juice." Especially helpful were Nan Schubel, Mary K. Erie, Valerie Andrews, Zorland Katz, Gene Busnar, Susan Newman, Simon Barsky, Terry Wolf, and of course Don Hackett. Final and very special thanks goes to Dr. Ilona Vass for her unfailing help and encouragement.

CONTENTS

GETTING STRONG

PART I

1

I WAS A 120-POUND WEAKLING

One spring night in 1976, after finishing a three-mile jog, I went out to the airport to meet my parents. They greeted me warmly, commenting on how good I looked now that I was a runner. As my mother and I waited for the luggage, we talked about how fit I was and how different my life had become now that I was physically active. When her blue bag appeared on the carousel, I confidently bent over to lift it— and nearly ripped my arm off.

"What do you have in here—rocks?" I joked. In fact, she had several books in the bag, but it was not any fuller or heavier than a suitcase usually is. Still, it was a real struggle for me to carry the bag the whole length of the airline lobby, and I had to stop and put it down several times, switching hands each time. When we finally met my father and he took the bag from me and carried it (along with another bag!) out to a taxi, I didn't even pretend I wasn't relieved. A small, common incident which I didn't give too much thought to—until the following evening when I sat down to type a letter.

At the time, I was living in a typical Manhattan

apartment where there was no room for anything, let alone a permanent setup for a typewriter; so, as usual, I took my portable machine (thirty-five pounds) from the closet into the dining area and set it up on the table. Though I didn't have to stop and put it down on my journey of maybe ten feet, I did feel as though I were engaged in a monumental battle with all the inanimate forces of nature. My struggle seemed all the more frustrating when I thought of the way my boyfriend lifts the typewriter as if it were a pillow.

As for my "portable" sewing machine, which weighs over forty pounds, I had long since given up carrying it to the table—I just pulled it out of the closet as far as the nearest electrical outlet and then sat and sewed on the floor, working the foot pedal with my knee.

And yet I was unusually fit. I ran fifteen miles a week, walked a lot, and played paddle ball out in my neighborhood schoolyard every Sunday afternoon. It was paddle ball that finally made me realize the source of my helplessness. During a hotly contested game with my boyfriend, I wound up throwing my paddle onto the concrete, chipping it, and screaming, "Don't you know I can't return backhand shots? What kind of a game can we have? I have no strength in my arms!"

And that was it, of course. Though all my life I had been dimly aware of my relative lack of strength, I had somehow never tied it in to all those inconveniences—major and minor—it had caused me. These ranged from my struggles with heavy objects to my nonexistent backhand to such simple frustrations as trying to open a stuck jar of olives.

Finally I faced it: I was a 120-pound weakling. But what to do about it? Well, I could always move into a larger apartment, give up paddle ball, and stop eating olives—but it seemed more practical to try to become stronger.

I knew from experience that improving my own muscular strength was possible. Before I had started running, my legs had been flabby and pockmarked. But after only a few months of running, my thighs and calves had developed muscles which, when flexed, were hard as rocks and which were able to stand up to hours of walking and running. My upper-body strength would, I reasoned, similarly improve from a systematic program of using the muscles.

From my readings on the subject of physical fitness I knew that weight lifting was one of the best ways to build strength, and the more I thought about it, the more it seemed as if that might be the answer. I had never heard of a woman lifting weights, but there seemed to be no reason why I couldn't give it a try. Since my legs had not become bulgy or overdeveloped from running, but instead firm and smooth and more shapely, I had no fears that I would turn into a muscle-bound lady gorilla.

Armed with my new curiosity, I went to the local Y and enrolled in a weight-lifting course. The night of the first class, I was astonished and delighted to find, along with the dozen men signed up, one other woman. Diane had enrolled for a specific reason: she was a serious squash player and wanted to improve her game. But she agreed with me that lack of strength in her everyday life was driving her crazy.

Our instructor was a little nervous but very pleased to see women enrolled in his class, though he admitted he wasn't sure exactly how to run a course for women. We agreed that we would just do the program he advocated for men, only using lighter weights. The first session was devoted to a general explanation of weight lifting and what it does, and as the talk continued, Diane and I grew increasingly dismayed.

Though we learned many excellent principles, all the instructor's discussion of "lats" and "muscle definition" was confusing and didn't seem related to what we were there for, which was simply to become stronger. From the comments of the men in the class, it became increasingly clear to us that most of them already possessed a considerable measure of strength and were taking the course primarily to help build beautiful he-man bodies.

When we went to the weight room to run through sample exercises, Diane and I grew even more discouraged. Crowded with grunting, bulging, glistening bodies, the room was obviously a fortress of male supremacy. The glances we drew ranged from amused to mocking to hostile. And when we tried to do some of the exercises, using the very lightest weights available, the problem was compounded: the weights, which most of the men in the course lifted easily, were too heavy for us! As we walked back to the women's locker room, Diane and I agreed that it had been a good idea, but neither of us could face going into that room again.

So a class in weight lifting wasn't the answer. But from the things the instructor had told us about training principles, I was still convinced that weights might be the key to strength improvement. I went to my neighborhood bookstore to see what books there might be on the topic.

I was very surprised, with books on fitness overflowing the shelves, to find *nothing* on the simple building of strength. Almost all the books gave general conditioning programs which deemphasized strength, at least for women. As for the books specifically on weight lifting, all of them took the same approach as the instructor in my weight-lifting course: lifting weights was a great way to look like Mr. America.

Still, I bought some weight-lifting books, then went to the library and began reading in the physiology section. As I continued to study, I realized that weight lifting was not only a way to get stronger, but also probably the best and fastest way. Further, I found that there were well-established methods of going about weight lifting. The only real obstacle to my starting was my lack of equipment. I couldn't face going back to that sweaty meat room again, and in any case I could barely handle the lightest weights there (about 10 pounds). But I thought I could handle weights of five pounds or less, and there were many objects around the house of that weight.

Applying the principles I had learned, I put together a simple strength-building program which was based on (but not limited to) lifting light weights. My weights were cans of peas and tomato juice, plastic bottles of detergent and spring water, and my electric iron.

And so I began my program. It didn't go smoothly at first. My main problem was not so much that my substitute weights were awkward to hold (which they were), but that they were too heavy. I kept revising my beginning weights downward to the point where one exercise, done with a one-pound can, was still a strain!

Another obstacle was my friends, who not only couldn't understand why I wanted to become strong, but made fun of my "pumping tomato juice" (which even I had to admit was much less glamorous than pumping iron, as in the movie of that title).

Finally, even though the idea of the program was exciting, the exercises themselves weren't much fun because they hurt. The program required a lot of effort, even though the total amount of time expended was just fifteen minutes three times a week. And afterwards my muscles would ache. I consoled myself by visualizing those sore muscles getting strong. And they did—not gradually, but rapidly. After doing the program only two times, I had increased the amount of weight I could use for most exercises. And each exercise session after that brought further improvements—sometimes dramatic, sometimes slight. These steady improvements made the workouts more fun, because it was exciting to watch the progress: where at first I had been exhausted by lifting two pounds three times for a given exercise, suddenly I could lift that weight five times; or I could lift a heavier weight the same number of times.

The increase in strength was beginning to show in my daily life. My first indication that the program worked came only two and a half weeks after I started, when I beat my boyfriend in two consecutive games of paddle ball, almost entirely because I was accurately and powerfully returning shots hit to my backhand. This change in my game was so dramatic that I thought it might be a fluke, but I went on to win games against several other opponents during the next few days.

The following week I bought some new furniture and had to rearrange my bedroom. Objects which had defeated me when I was moving in were now, if not easy to move, at least manageable without help. Even my typewriter was beginning to seem truly portable. I was getting strong! And this after a total of just ten sessions.

I could hardly wait for new developments—and they came, sometimes in surprising ways. For instance, a friend whom I often run with commented, "You know what? Your shoulders look different."

"What do you mean, different?" I asked.

"Better—less bony. What have you been doing?"

When I finished my run, I looked in the mirror. It was true: my shoulders *were* less bony, and so was my back, which had always had "angel wings"—shoulder blades sticking out. The change was not to broader shoulders or bulging muscles, but to smoothness and a better contour, and I had lost my stooped look—a common occupational hazard of writers. My forearms, too, were changing shape: instead of the matchsticks they had always resembled, they were now gently rounded.

Finally, and surprisingly, I discovered that I felt much better physically after starting my program. Most days I spend so much time at a desk that I have a tendency to get stiff and sore. Although I can't say that this problem disappeared altogether as a result of getting strong, I found after several weeks that I could work longer hours at my desk with less fatigue, at least in part because my posture had improved, as had the endurance of all my muscles. My flexibility, too, was greater. After two months on my program, I attended a yoga class and found that I was able to hold many postures longer and in more extreme positions than previously, even though I had not been practicing yoga for months.

So, in only twelve weeks, I not only had become much stronger, I had also improved my figure and general well-being. Best of all, I was able to maintain my new level of strength by exercising only once or twice a week. The exercises, which had been difficult at first, became easier and more pleasant week by week.

What about you? By following the program in this book almost any woman can achieve the results I did—without buying a thing, or even leaving her own home. You don't need any skill or previous training to do the program—all it takes is fifteen minutes or so three times a week, the willingness to exert some effort, and the desire to get strong.

2

WHY BE STRONG?

A Nation of Weak Sisters

It's not news that Americans are sports crazy. With increasing awareness of the importance of physical activity, we are changing from a nation of spectators to a nation of participants, and growing numbers of these new athletes are female. In suburbs, cities, and the country, women are taking to the tennis courts, the tracks, the bicycle paths. And by and large, these women are becoming more fit as they become more athletic, with the stamina to run or bike for miles, the coordination and skill to play several sets of tennis, and the flexibility to maintain a full lotus through twenty minutes of yoga meditation. But in one important area of physical fitness most American women are still in the age of waist-cinchers and bustles: we have no strength, particularly upper-body strength.

Traditionally, no one cared or even noticed that women were not strong. After all, who needed a female piano mover? But as more and more women get into sports, it becomes more and more noticeable. Take the experience of my friend Janet, who is a year-round outdoors enthusiast. Though in the winter she has the stamina to go cross-country skiing for hours on end, in the summer she finds she needs help lifting a canoe, which most of the men she knows can do easily.

Even women who aren't interested in sports are reminded of their lack of strength every time they have to lift a typewriter or a tape recorder or pick up a struggling, growing baby. And what about the little frustrations of life that plague almost all of us at one time or another? "I'll tell you what gets me," says my neighbor Phyllis. "It's going on trips. By now I've learned not to pack much, but then I never have the clothes I need when I go somewhere." And how many of us have dropped and broken a heavy jar because we lacked the grip strength to hold on to it? Grip strength, in fact, is considered an important measure of overall body strength by physiologists— and it's one of the areas in which women are notoriously weak.

Apart from the frustrations and sometimes serious inconveniences caused by inadequate upper-body strength, lack of strength can also lead to injuries. A recent survey of college physical education departments revealed that female athletes suffered far more injuries than their male counterparts, and that lack of precollege conditioning was a major factor in these injuries. The great tennis champion Billie Jean King has said that she probably wouldn't have suffered the constant knee problems that have plagued her career if she had lifted weights her whole life. And doctors report that many back injuries and strains caused by lifting heavy objects could have been avoided had the victim possessed adequate back and shoulder strength.

Lack of strength is even a factor in some types of job discrimination. Minimal-strength standards for fire fighting and police work have in the past prevented many otherwise qualified women from entering these careers (though there are many other discriminatory forces operating here as well). And what about the young woman who wanted to be a movie projectionist but was disqualified because of an archaic rule which stated that all projectionists had to be able to lift a thirty-five-pound projector over their heads?

So far I haven't told you anything new. Everyone knows that women are "the weaker sex." It is only very recently, however, that it has become apparent just how much weaker.

The West Point Studies

As the whole world knows by now, the summer of 1976 marked a momentous event: for the first time in its 174-year history, the United States Military Academy was forced to open its doors to women. Naturally, the hallowed institution was thrown into a panic. New facilities would have to be built, modifications of programs would have to be made—but what sort of modifications, and in what areas? Perhaps the greatest consternation was felt in the Office of Physical Education, which is responsible for the rigorous physical training of all new cadets. Traditionally, the first summer at West Point is a grueling sink-or-swim round of daily hard runs, rifle drills, calisthenics, obstacle courses. Many of the incoming men are former high school athletes, and most of them quickly adjust to the routine. But what about the women?

"When we started, we had no idea what to do," says Dr. Robert Stauffer, Director of Research for the Point's "Project Summertime." "We knew the women wouldn't be up to the men—but we didn't know what modifications to make." A search of the literature was no help, because there were few studies on women's strength, and those few had little correlation to studies on men. Ultimately, West Point decided to use the first group of women as guinea pigs, putting them through the same routines as the men and carefully following and evaluating the performance of thirty women cadets, compared to that of thirty men. These sixty cadets were tested before and after the summer conditioning program to determine what modifications would have to be made in the future.

The results were shocking.

"It was devastating," says Dr. Stauffer. "It almost appeared that West Point had set up the tests so the women would fail."

How badly did the women do? Well, even though these were healthy young women, many of them former high school varsity athletes, out of 127 women, only one was strong enough to pass the minimal entrance requirements for men. Furthermore, in terms of overall fitness, ninety-eight percent of the women were below the least-fit male cadets. The top two percent of the women overlapped with the *bottom* two percent of the men! This was true in all areas of fitness, but particularly in upper-body strength. At the end of the summer, things were not much better. Although most of the women had improved slightly in all areas, the only significant improvement was in cardiovascular fitness, which now equaled that of the men cadets.

Specifically, the areas of greatest weakness for the women were arm and shoulder strength (which is measured by the ability to do pushups and pullups) and grip strength (which depends on the muscles of the forearm). The women also had poorly developed trunk muscles (back and abdomen); they were unable to keep their bodies straight during pushups, and were awkward in running and jumping, because these muscles are very important for stabilizing the pelvis.

Muscular endurance, another measure of physical fitness, was also very poor among the women. According to Dr. Stauffer, the women "were at a great disadvantage when they had to perform any repetitive exercises, such as pushups or rifle drill."

Future generations of women cadets will of course profit from the experiences of the first: they will, for example, be permitted to do the daily runs in running shoes, to cut down on injuries caused by running in heavy combat boots. More important, instead of being thrown into rifle drill and calisthenics without any preparation, the women will first be taken through gradual, progressive weight-lifting exercises to improve their endurance and strength.

Dr. James A. Peterson, the physical education director of the training program, believes the new emphasis on training should make a significant difference in the women's performance, though no one expects them to become as strong as the men. Both Dr. Peterson and Dr. Stauffer believe that there is little limit to women's physical *potential*, but, as Dr. Stauffer ruefully puts it, "It's just impossible to change the first seventeen years of someone's life in one summer."

Women and Strength

When Dr. Stauffer speaks of the first seventeen years of a woman's life, he is also talking about the cultural conditioning, subtle and not so subtle, which teaches us that it's not necessary or desirable for women to be strong. Because of this bias, strength-building exercises such as pushups and weight training are not emphasized in girls' physical education programs, as they are in boys'. When I was in high school most of the courses I took in gym emphasized such "ladylike" abilities as posture and balance, while the boys I knew were learning how to chin themselves and climb ropes.

Even when similar courses are offered to both sexes, the emphasis in teaching is different. In both team sports and individual activities, boys are encouraged to push themselves to the limit, while girls are generally allowed to drop out when they've had enough. And it's still a nearly universal practice in this country to excuse girls from gym classes on the days they're having their period—whether they feel sick or not. Thus, boys learn that maximum exertion and even pain are a necessary part of physical activity, while girls learn to avoid exertion and the pain it sometimes brings. While no sensible person would agree with the stereotyped coach's attitude of "Let's all die for Haywood High," our feminine reluctance to meet physical challenges has largely been responsible for our remaining second-class citizens in fitness. Dr. Peterson feels that this is one of the most important reasons for the great physical differences between the men and women cadets, and he tells the young men who are in charge of new cadets to push the women just as hard as they do the men. "They might resent it at first," he says, "but later they'll realize it was for their own good."

Though Dr. Peterson's advice might seem cruel, it isn't, really. The fact is that the pain of physical exertion is not the same kind of pain as that, say, from an injury or a toothache, but most women don't know this, because they have been inactive for so much of their lives.

Any woman seeking to end that inactivity and improve her strength, however, will find very little practical help. Even such excellent fitness programs as the Canadian Air Force Exercises start out with the bias that assumes that upper-body strength is not important for women. Compare almost any system of exercise designed for both men and women, and you will find that the goals for the two sexes are quite different. This contrast became evident to me when I took a calisthenics class at my local Y. Though several exercises which do promote upper-body strength were included, such as chinups and pushups, the women in the class were excused from these because most of us simply couldn't do them. Rather than give us remedial strength-building exercises, the instructors simply encouraged the women to keep active by bending or twisting, while the men worked on increasing their strength!

These cultural expectations ensure that women's weakness, like men's superior strength, is maintained throughout their lives. The main reason most men can lift heavy things is that they *do* lift heavy things—from the time they are children. This constant use of already trained muscles helps to maintain strength, while women tend to become less and less active as their muscles become weaker and weaker.

But, you may say, so what if I'm not strong? Even if I find that I can't carry my own suitcase or open a window, I can always get a man to do it for me.

Well, for one thing, while it may be nice to have a man carrying your suitcases and lifting heavy objects, there may not be a man around to do it all the time—or even, for many of today's women, most of the time. As more and more women live alone and travel alone, it becomes necessary simply as a practical matter to be able to lift and carry things without help.

Moreover, some men are beginning to rebel at their traditional roles. "You're so liberated; carry it yourself" is a not-uncommon remark. A married friend of mine pointed out recently that he sometimes feels his wife and daughters take him along on shopping trips as a "beast of burden—they won't even *try* to carry their own things." (While I sympathize with my friend, I suspect that he has contributed to his own problem by not encouraging his daughters to develop strength. He plays ball with his son—but not his daughters [throwing promotes arm and shoulder strength]. And I'm reminded of the children of a close friend of mine, ages six and seven, who are equally active, bright, and attractive. While they engage in many of the same activities, I have noticed that on the playground Christine usually plays on the swings while Matthew is chinning himself.)

A more common argument against building upper-body strength is that it's not considered "ladylike" to have strong, bulging muscles. But developing strength does *not* mean developing bulging muscles—not for women, anyway. According to the studies that have been done (and my own experience), women can greatly increase their strength without any visible increase in muscle mass. Luckily for us, a hormonal factor limits the size to which a woman's muscles can grow—though there is no corresponding limit to the increase in strength.

In fact, not only will a program of strength building not produce a set of bulging muscles, it will actually improve your figure. After a few sessions of working out, you will probably find that the contours of your body have become smoother, slimmer, and better defined. Even if you don't lose weight, you will at least look slimmer, and any pockets of flab will be reduced, because the areas are developing muscle tone. This is particularly true of the upper arms. One of the most underused muscles on most women's bodies is the triceps—the muscle at the back of the upper arm. If you are suffering from sag—or incipient sag—here, getting strong is the fastest way to tighten up.

As you improve your abdominal strength, your stomach will become flatter and your waist may appear smaller. Many women who have trained with weights, both on this program and at gyms, have reported an increase in bust size. This is most evident in women who are very small-breasted, but more generously endowed women too have noticed that their breasts appear firmer and higher as the underlying pectoral muscles become strong and well developed.

So-called "cellulite" will also begin to disappear as you work on getting strong. Cellulite is actually just flab, which in some women appears as wrinkled, pocked areas on certain parts of the body. If you get rid of excess fat (see Chapter Nine) and replace it with firm muscle, the wrinkled, pocked areas will vanish. The stronger you become, in fact, the less you will have to worry about cellulite, flab, or sagging in any area.

You will also find that it is easier to get through your daily life. You'll be able to carry heavy bags home from the supermarket without fear of dropping them and breaking the eggs. If something falls behind a heavy chair, you won't have to wait for someone to help you move it. You won't be victimized by stuck jar lids; and any repetitive chore, such as washing walls, will seem easier, because the endurance of your muscles will be greater.

Getting strong even feels good. It feels good to take muscles through their range of motion and use them the way they were meant to be used. As you progress through the program, you'll notice a growing awareness of your body and all its muscles, and you'll feel a sense of pride in knowing that your body is the best it can be—for you.

Finally, getting strong provides profound psychological benefits—benefits which are especially important for women. Most of the women in the studies on strength building report an increased feeling of security about their own bodies—which correlates with a sense of security in the world.

This sense of security includes but is not limited to a lessening of the physical fear that so many women, particularly those living in cities, often feel. While no one in her right mind would try to fight off a 180-pound man who is armed with a switchblade, just the knowledge that you are fit and strong can make it psychologically more comfortable to walk down a city street at night. In fact, studies have shown that the most likely victims of muggers and rapists are those people who look and appear fearful, who visibly lack self-confidence and feel themselves to be potential victims. While getting strong will not make you immune to attack by weirdos and criminals, it may help you to *feel* like less of a victim and therefore actually reduce your chances of being victimized.

This level of confidence can carry into areas other than physical security. In my own case, getting strong has proved to me that I am in control of my body— and, by implication, in control of all the other parts of my life. Rightly or wrongly, I now feel that I can do almost anything that I set out to do. For example, not long after I began my strength-building program I bought a dimmer switch for the lamp in my living room. A couple of men I know had promised to install it for me, but somehow neither ever had the time. When the switch still wasn't installed two days before a dinner party I'd been planning, I began to get angry at my friends. I was rearranging some furniture in preparation for the party when I suddenly stopped and thought: "Wait a minute. Here I am moving heavy furniture around, and I'm afraid of a lousy light switch? I'm not a moron; I can follow printed instructions. I'm sick and tired of being helpless, and I'm going to install that switch myself!"

Since I had never done any wiring in my life, it

took me all afternoon. But with the help of my Swiss Army knife and manicure scissors I did install the switch. It looked fine, and it worked perfectly.

The key here was the thought: "I'm sick and tired of being helpless." Of course, I'm not helpless and never have been, but it took my venture into strength building to prove that to myself.

For too many years, women have been told that they can't do things. "You can't understand math; you can't run for office; you can't climb Mt. Everest." Nonsense. As women all over the world are beginning to demonstrate, you can do almost anything you want to if you have confidence in yourself. And the best way to start building your own confidence is by building your strength.

The strength-building program I've developed can be done by any woman in her own home or apartment (or in a gym, if you prefer). There's nothing you need to buy—as you will see, you can use objects which you probably already have around the house—though if you emphasize the weight-training part of the program, you may wish to buy an inexpensive dumbbell set after a few weeks.

If you want a complete conditioning program, this book is not for you. But if you want to improve your strength for sports or for coping with life's hassles— or if you simply want a fast and effective way to streamline your figure—then turn the page and start getting strong.

3

YOU AND YOUR BODY

What Is Fitness?

Physical fitness means different things to different people: to some it is a current fad; to others it's the ability to jog seven miles or do two hundred pushups; to many it is simply freedom from illness. According to the *Physical Fitness Research Digest*, published by the President's Council on Physical Fitness and Sports, physical fitness is "the ability to carry out daily tasks with vigor and alertness, without undue fatigue, and with ample energy to enjoy leisure-time pursuits and to meet unusual situations and unforeseen emergencies." In other words, physical fitness is the ability to lead an active, effective, and enjoyable life.

There are growing indications that the physically fit may live longer, and in any case it is true that they tend to age more slowly: the more active a person is, the less likely she is to develop such "diseases" of aging as osteoporosis (brittle bones) and atherosclerosis (hardening of the arteries), as well as stiffness and atrophied muscles.

There are several components to this general quality we call physical fitness. These include cardiovascular fitness, flexibility, and muscular strength and endurance.

By far the most important of these is cardiovascular fitness. This very important criterion of fitness refers to the health and strength of your heart and circulatory and respiratory systems. Cardiovascular fitness is achieved by engaging in "aerobic" exercises, which are strenuous, rhythmic activities in which you breathe deeply, your heart beats fast, and you perspire. The four basic aerobic exercises are running, walking, swimming, and bicycling (though many other activities as well tend to be aerobic).

Since this is a book on building muscular strength, there isn't room to go into a detailed discussion of cardiovascular fitness and aerobic exercises here, beyond this very important point: IF YOU HAVE THE TIME OR INCLINATION TO ENGAGE IN ONLY ONE KIND OF SPORT OR EXERCISE REGIMEN, IT SHOULD BE AN AEROBIC SPORT OR EXERCISE.

So go out and jog, swim, walk, or bike. There are many excellent books to help you learn how to approach aerobic exercise; all of them stress that you should start slowly and gradually build up the level of exertion—the more gradually the older or more out of shape you are. (See the Selected Bibliography for a list of books on aerobic exercises.)

On the other hand, if you are already aerobically fit or are thinking of beginning an aerobic program, you will probably want, as I did, to improve every aspect of your total fitness. Which leads us to the next components of physical fitness: flexibility and muscular strength and endurance.

Flexibility has to do primarily with the mobility of your joints. Gentle stretching exercises such as yoga asanas help to promote this kind of fitness, and flexibility exercises should be included as a part of any kind of exercise regimen. In general, women tend to be much more flexible than men—which is fine, up to a point. Too much flexibility without corresponding muscular strength can lead to joint injuries such as dislocations or torn cartilage, tendons, or ligaments. (Too little flexibility can also lead to injuries—the kind often suffered by very muscular football players.)

The muscular side of fitness has two aspects: muscular strength and muscular endurance. Strength is measured by the ability of your muscles to perform work; that is, to raise or lower a given amount of weight or to resist a given amount of pressure. Muscular endurance refers to the ability of a muscle to perform a given task for an extended period of time. Lifting a weight of one hundred pounds once shows strength; lifting the same weight thirty-five times shows endurance.

Muscular strength and endurance are important in women's lives, and most women have far too little of both. Strength is what enables you to cope with day-to-day activities and sudden emergencies (carrying a heavy briefcase to the office or catching a toddler who has just stepped out of his high chair); endurance prepares you to hold up when you have to perform repetitious work (painting a ceiling or cleaning out a closet).

There are various ways to increase muscular strength and endurance, but before we examine them, let's take a closer look at those muscles we're trying to improve.

You and Your Muscles

Picture a medieval castle surrounded by a moat and reachable only by a drawbridge. When the castle is under attack, the residents of the castle pull up the drawbridge, which is attached to a long cable, until it is shut and the castle is safe.

Your muscles work in much the same way as that cable. Their job is to move your skeleton around, and they do it by pulling on your bones. Continuing the analogy, imagine your forearm as the drawbridge and your muscle as the cable. When you want to raise your forearm to your shoulder, a signal goes out to your arm muscle from your brain, and the muscle shortens in response. As it shortens, it pulls on the bone of your forearm and lifts it, just as that cable lifted the drawbridge. When you want to lower your forearm, a signal goes out to another muscle, which pulls on the bone in the opposite direction, while the first muscle relaxes.

Though the above example is greatly simplified for purposes of illustration, the muscles in your body (with some exceptions) work very much like that cable. For most actions, several of your muscles work together to produce the movement; furthermore, most muscles have more than one function. When you are engaged in any activity, even sitting or just standing around, your muscles are constantly contracting (shortening) and extending (lengthening) to balance your body against the forces of gravity. These movements are automatic, and you usually aren't even aware they are going on, but without them your body would collapse like a sack of bones. Thus, poor posture is generally a result of poor muscular strength or of an imbalance in the relative strength of different muscle groups.

Most exercise books and programs don't tell you much about your muscles, so it may be a mystery why a certain exercise is prescribed. Also, if you are to do an exercise properly, it helps to understand where the involved muscle is and what it is supposed to do. You may want to get stronger to improve your backhand, but how can you do that unless you know which muscles are involved in hitting that backhand?

The following is a brief description of some of the major muscles in your body and what they do.

For our purposes, we can divide the muscles into five groups: those of the upper body (neck, shoulders, chest and upper back), the arms, the abdomen, the hips and lower back, and the legs. Although every muscle group contains many separate muscles, each with its own name, I will refer to the entire muscle group by the name most commonly used in weight-training books. In most cases, this refers to the largest muscle in each group.

1. UPPER-BODY MUSCLES

Neck muscles. Your neck muscles are responsible for moving your head from front to back and from side to side, and for protecting your upper spinal cord from injury. You can feel the working of your neck muscles by putting your hand on the side of your neck and bending your head from side to side. Sports in which neck strength is extremely important include soccer and wrestling.

Shoulder muscles. This important group, the deltoid muscles, covers your shoulders, top, sides, front and back. The shoulder muscles are responsible for raising your arms to the front or side and upward. To feel these muscles work, place the palm of one hand over the opposite shoulder, then raise your arm straight out and up. The deltoids are involved in all daily activities which involve raising your arms, and in such sports as tennis, golf, archery and swimming.

Chest muscles. If you've ever done exercises to firm your bust, then you know about the pectoral mus-

cles, which are located on the sides and center of your
chest, underneath your breasts. The main purpose of
your pectoral muscles is to move your arms across
your body. They also assist in pushing your arms out
in front, and they work with the shoulder muscles in
such activities as throwing. When you clasp your
hands together and squeeze as tightly as you can, as
in those breast-development exercises, you are contracting the pectoral muscles. To feel the pectorals
working, lie on your back with one arm stretched out
to the side, a light weight held in that hand. Put the
opposite hand on the side of your breast near your
armpit, then raise the outstretched arm straight up
and toward the center of your body. As the arm moves,
you should feel the pectoral muscles contracting.

The pectorals are essential in daily activities which
involve holding large objects, and in any pushing
movements, such as mowing the lawn or moving a
piece of furniture. And of course if you have strong,
firm pectorals, you will have a higher, firmer bust line,
since the breast tissue is supported by these muscles.
Sports in which pectoral strength is important include tennis, swimming, golf, and any sport which
involves throwing.

Upper-back muscles. There are two important
upper-back muscle groups, the trapezius (traps) and
latissimus dorsi (lats). The traps are triangular-shaped
muscles which cover virtually all of your upper back.
The main functions of your traps are to raise your
shoulders upward, as in a shrug, and to rotate your
shoulders for various arm movements. This very strong
muscle also protects your neck and shoulders from
injury. To feel your traps working, put your hands on
the upper part of your back behind your shoulders,
and shrug.

Your lats are located on the sides of your upper
back, just below the traps. Their main purpose is to

assist your arm muscles when you are pulling your arms toward the body. Most women have very weak lats, which is why most of us cannot do chinups and rope climbs. The lats are involved in such activities as pulling down a stuck window and are extremely important in swimming. To feel your lats, raise one arm straight up in the air, and put the palm of your opposite hand on the side of your back, an inch or two below the armpit. Lower the upraised arm by bending your elbow. As your arm approaches your body, you should feel the muscle contracting.

Both upper-back muscle groups are used in such sports as tennis, golf, swimming, rowing, fencing, archery, and any activity involving throwing.

2. ARM MUSCLES

Back of upper arm. This muscle, which makes up two-thirds of your upper arm, is called the triceps. Like the lats, the triceps are extremely underdeveloped in most women, and that is one reason we all tend to get saggy in the upper arm by our late twenties. The main purposes of the triceps are to straighten your arm and to assist in pushing movements away from your body. To feel your triceps working, extend one arm straight out in front of you, with the opposite hand on the back of your arm. Now forcefully straighten your elbow as strongly as you can, and you will feel the triceps move. The triceps comes into play in daily activities which involve lifting things over your head (such as putting a casserole pan into a high cupboard), or extending your arms in any direction; it is important in swimming, throwing, basketball, and fencing.

Front of upper arm. The biceps are muscles on the fronts of your upper arms. Their main purpose is to bend your elbow, and they are used in any lifting movement in which your arm is bent, as well as in any pulling movement (they work together with your lats and deltoids). To see your biceps, stand in front of a mirror and make a fist with your arm bent; or place your fingertips over the front of your upper arm and bend and straighten your elbow to feel this muscle move. Sports in which biceps strength is important include archery, swimming, and gymnastics.

Forearm muscles. The muscles of your forearm are responsible for moving your wrist and for gripping. To feel your forearm muscles work, hold a ball in one hand and circle that forearm with the other hand, just below the elbow. Now squeeze the ball. The forearm muscles are used in almost all daily activities, as well as in sports in which grip strength is important, such as racket sports, golf, handball, fishing, and baseball.

3. ABDOMINAL MUSCLES

Your abdominal muscles are located in the center and along the sides of your abdomen. The central muscles are primarily responsible for bending your trunk forward, while the side muscles enable you to turn your trunk from side to side, as well as to bend from the side. In addition, these very important muscles aid in posture, in stabilizing your trunk during activity, and in holding your internal organs in place.

The easiest and most startling way to feel your abdominal muscles at work is to lie on your back, knees bent, with your hands over your abdomen. Now slowly curl up to a sitting position. Even if you only lift your neck and head off the floor, you will feel a strong tightening in your abdomen.

Your abdominal muscles are used in all activities and all sports. Strong abdominal muscles are essential for women who plan to have children.

4. HIP AND LOWER-BACK MUSCLES

The muscles of your lower back are responsible for straightening your trunk when you are in a bent-over position; they are thus extremely important in maintaining posture. Running is a good way to build strength in this area, which is one of the most ignored muscle groups of the body. To feel your lower-back muscles, stand up with your fingertips on your lower back. Now bend *slightly* forward from the waist, then back.

Like the abdominal muscles, the lower-back muscles come into play in all daily activities. They are especially important in sports such as swimming, golf, and tennis.

5. LEG MUSCLES

Buttocks. Many women tend to regard the buttocks as something to be jammed into a girdle or reduced through any means at all. Though many of us carry a lot of body fat there, underneath the fat is the largest and strongest muscle group of the body. The main function of the buttocks muscles is to move your thighs toward the back. To get a sense of how this works, stand with one hand on a chair back for balance and with the other hand on your buttocks. Now slowly raise your leg straight out in back. The higher you lift your leg, the more of a tightening you should feel. The action of the buttocks muscles is essential in walking, running, and dancing, and in sports such as skiing, skating, swimming, biking, football, and soccer.

Front of thigh. The quadriceps is a large muscle group located on the front of your thigh. Its main function is to straighten your knee. You can feel the quadriceps by sitting with your hand on the front of your thigh toward the knee, and then straightening the knee. This muscle group is extremely important in any activity requiring walking, running, jumping, or kicking.

Back of thigh. The muscle group located on the back of your thighs is called the hamstrings. The hamstrings' main function is to bend your knees. To feel the hamstrings working, stand with your hand on the back of one thigh and bend your lower leg up toward your buttocks. This muscle group is important in many of the same activities as the quadriceps; athletes who engage in sports which require a great deal of running sometimes develop tight hamstrings. Tight hamstrings are an important cause of lower-back pain; this is especially common in women who don't exercise.

Calf muscles. These muscles are located on the backs of your lower legs. The main purpose is to lift your heel off the floor. Without them, you wouldn't be able to walk. You can see your calf muscles working by standing sideways in front of a full-length mirror and rising on your toes: the calf muscle will bulge as it shortens, then lengthen again as you lower yourself. After years of wearing high-heeled shoes, women tend to have shortened, inflexible calf muscles, which can sometimes cause ankle pain. The calves are obviously important in any daily activity which requires mobility, and in sports such as sprinting, hurdling, and mountain climbing, as well as in all sports which involve jumping.

Although most women tend to be weaker in certain muscles than in others, each of us develops strength and endurance in different areas just from everyday activities. For example, a woman who spends a great deal of time carrying a baby around will tend to develop her shoulders, chest, and biceps (at least on one side) more than a woman who doesn't carry a baby around; a woman who regularly walks to work will have *relatively* stronger lower-back and leg muscles, and someone who brushes her hair one hundred strokes a day will develop a strong forearm.

Simply relying on daily activity—or even on one sport such as tennis—will not develop all muscles equally; only a strength-building program which exercises all the major muscle groups can do that. There are three types of exercise which build muscular strength and endurance.

Isometric, Isotonic, and Isokinetic Exercises

You may have heard of isometric exercises. They were greatly in fashion a few years ago when men were invited to double their muscle strength and bulk in a few minutes a day by performing exercises which took only six to ten seconds each. These exercises involved contracting a muscle in a static position for a few seconds—for example, if you press your arm against a wall, the muscle is contracting, but it isn't going anywhere. And this is the main drawback to isometric exercises. While they work—those men who performed the exercises did build bigger, stronger muscles—they work best only in the position in which the exercise is being performed. In other words, if you press against a wall with your arm for ten seconds a day, your muscles will become much stronger —but mostly when it is called upon to perform an action in which it is in the same general position as when it was pushing against the wall—although it does gain some strength throughout its whole range of motion.

This shortcoming of isometric exercises can be partly compensated for by performing the exercise with the muscle held in several different positions, but this complicates the exercise routine. Also, performing isometric exercises may be dangerous to some people with high blood pressure.

The limitations of isometric exercises can be overcome by exercising a muscle throughout its range of motion: for example, if you lift a weight from shoulder height to over your head, fully extending your arms, the muscles involved get the chance to shorten fully as they draw the arms up. When you lower the weight, the same muscles lengthen fully. The two types of exercise which work muscles in this way are known as isotonic and isokinetic exercises.

Isokinetic exercises are performed on machines which provide a constant resistance against the muscle as it goes through its whole range of motion. The best-known isokinetic machine is the Nautilus, said to produce greatly increased strength in a short period of time. The drawbacks to isokinetic exercises are, obviously, that machines are needed (they are very large and expensive) and that one generally has to join a health club to gain access to them.

Isotonic exercises are those in which you raise or lower a weight through the range of motion of a muscle. Most of life's activities are performed with isotonic muscular contractions. You are doing an isotonic movement every time you pick up the telephone to make a call, or indeed when you perform any muscular activity (whether you are holding something or not), because your muscles are moving the weight of your body. The prime examples of isotonic exercises are, not surprisingly, calisthenics and weight lifting. You are probably already familiar with such calisthenic exercises as pullups and situps, in which the weight of your body acts as resistance to your muscles;

in weight training, you add more resistance by manipulating free-standing objects.

Women with a special need for greatly increased strength in some area—for a particular sport, say, or for recovering from an injury—can probably make the best and most rapid progress by working out on an isokinetic machine. But for the vast majority of women, a simple program making use of calisthenics and free-standing weights is all that's needed to get strong.

Weight Training—What It Is and Isn't

Weight lifting, body building, and weight training —these confusing terms, often used interchangeably, actually refer to three separate things: the first is a competitive sport, the second an esthetic competition, and the last a system of exercise.

When you hear the term "weight lifting," what image comes to mind? If you're like me and many other Americans, it is that of Vasily Alexeev, the Olympic Gold Medal champion from the USSR. The picture of his performance in the 1976 Olympics is unforgettable: a man who makes King Kong look puny walking confidently onto the Olympic weight-lifting stage, the bulk of his muscles bulging and rippling, his gigantic abdomen barely held in by his tent-sized leotard. Then Alexeev bends and grasps a weight of unimaginable poundage and slowly, slowly, clearly straining, lifts it up and over his head, where he holds it, grunting and sweating in triumph. Though this isn't the sort of sport that I can imagine watching on a regular basis, the magnificence of Alexeev's effort kept me glued to the TV set. I'm sure he could lift a Volkswagen if he put his mind to it.

Weight lifting is a competitive sport. Its participants spend a great deal of time lifting progressively heavier weights with the aim of lifting even heavier weights. Increasing the amount of weight the participant can handle is the goal of the training. Weight lifters include competitive athletes in high school and college, as well as Olympic weight lifters like Alexeev who do only a very few carefully prescribed lifts in international competition (though they must work out using many other exercises than those in competition). Most of the men in this sport have large, bulging muscles, leading in some cases to a rather grotesque appearance.

Though weight lifting is almost entirely a male sport, a very few women are beginning to enter it competitively. According to the AP, a 114-pound young woman named Terry Dillard set an Iowa weight-lifting record for both men and women by lifting 255 pounds!

Body building is not quite the same as weight lifting. Arnold Schwarzenegger, the likable star of the movie *Pumping Iron*, is the best-known example of a body builder as opposed to a weight lifter. Though body builders spend a great deal of time lifting extremely heavy weights, their goal is not to see how much weight they can lift, but rather to build up specific areas of their body for the sake of appearance.

A body builder may spend two to five hours each day lifting weights to develop certain muscles. In body-building competition, strength is not important, though body builders are very strong. What is important is how the men look: they display heavy, symmetrical muscular development, with each muscle clearly defined. I know few women who are attracted to that heavily muscled look, but this is a competition which is rapidly increasing in popularity. The most coveted awards in body building are Mr. America, Mr. USA, Mr. Universe, and Mr. World. The winner of a body-building contest is awarded the title of Most Muscular Man, but there are also consolation awards for Best Arms, Best Legs, Best Back, and in some cases Best Poser (though apparently there is no Mr. Congeniality). Instead of looking for a combination of grace, poise, and beauty, as in female beauty contests, body-building judges look for the best combination of muscle size and shape, absence of fat, symmetry, and general appearance.

Body building is entirely a male event, one it would be unthinkable for women to enter.

Weight training, the final category, is not a sport as such, but a system of exercise used by weight lifters, body builders, and many other athletes. The goals of weight training are to increase muscle tone, strength, and endurance, and to improve body contours. Studies have shown that weight training, using free-standing weights (barbells and dumbbells) or isokinetic machines, is the best, easiest, and fastest way to achieve each of these goals.

After years of experimentation, physiologists have found that weight training is most efficient when performed according to certain basic principles. The most important of these for our purposes are two: progressive resistance and overload.

The principle of overload is simply common sense: if you want to improve the strength of your muscles, you must ask them to do more work than they normally do. Suppose the heaviest sack of groceries you can comfortably carry one block weighs fifteen pounds and that you always limit yourself to carrying that amount that distance. It follows that you will never be able *comfortably* to carry a sack weighing fifteen pounds for more than one block, and you will never be able *comfortably* to carry one weighing sixteen pounds even one block. Anything much heavier or much farther will be not only uncomfortable but probably impossible for you.

To improve your grocery-sack-carrying ability, therefore, you must practice one of two things: carrying heavier sacks or carrying the same sack a little farther (or you may do both). For instance, you might practice carrying a sixteen-pound bag home from the grocery. That extra pound is the *overload*. At first you will find it difficult to go the whole block, and you may even have to stop and rest before you get home, because your muscles are only strong enough to carry a fifteen-pound sack. Quickly, however, your muscles will adjust to the increased work load, and soon you will find that it is now as easy to carry a sixteen-pound sack one block as it was to carry the fifteen-pound sack that distance. To further improve your strength, you might take a different route so that you are carrying the bag farther than one block. This is another form of overload, one designed to improve your endurance as well as your strength. In both cases, while the overload will be hard to handle at first, you will soon adjust to the new weight and/or distance.

But what if you want to be able to carry a twenty-five-pound bag of groceries? This brings us to the second principle, that of *progressive* resistance. This means that in order to continue increasing your strength, you must continue to add overloads on a regular basis. Going on with the example of the sack of groceries, you might now try to carry seventeen pounds, then eighteen, and so on, until twenty-five pounds becomes the weight that your muscles are used to. At this point twenty-five pounds is *not* an overload, and to further increase your strength you would have to add even more weight.

If twenty-five pounds is your goal, though, you may stop practicing (or training) and simply maintain your new strength. While the period of training, to be effective, requires working out at least three times a week, maintaining strength is much easier, and can be done by working out only once every week or two.

These two principles are the basis on which most weight-training programs rest: you start with a weight which you can lift a certain number of times, and then gradually and systematically increase the number of times and/or the amount of weight until your muscles adjust to the new work load. As you continue to progress, you continue to add weight (usually every workout will see an increase either in the number of times you lift or the amount of the weight) until you reach your own goals.

Benefits of Weight Training

Though the positive results of weight training have long been known and accepted by most male athletes, it is only fairly recently that women have started to train with weights; in many cases, the special benefits to women are still being discovered.

Although any conditioning program will improve your appearance and sports ability, weight training is the fastest way to achieve these goals. Not only does a weight-training program increase muscular strength and endurance, it can improve flexibility dramatically. In my case I was astonished to find after a few weeks on my strength-building program that my ability to do yoga asanas had improved, even though I hadn't been doing yoga regularly. It seems that the image of a stiff, muscle-bound weight lifter is just as much a myth as other popular ideas about weight training, such as the belief that women who lift weights will develop large, bulging muscles.

Dr. Jack Wilmore, a nationally known exercise physiologist, put that last myth to rest in a study of college-age men and women on a ten-week weight-training program. He found that the percentage of increase in strength for both groups was the same (though of course the women were starting from a point far behind the men), but that the increase in muscle bulk was much greater for the men. In fact, Wilmore found that the women generally developed only one-tenth the muscle mass of men of the same size on the same program. Even that might sound like a lot of muscle mass, but remember that the muscle is going to appear in places where you formerly had fat and flab—so your contours will remain approximately the same size or even smaller, while their appearance will be smoother, leaner, and firmer. That is, through a simple, dynamic program of weight training, most women can greatly increase their strength at the same time as they improve their overall appearance. Quite a two-for-one deal!

Before you go on and learn how to become strong, once again I want to urge you to try an aerobic activity if you are not now involved in any sort of exercise. You will find that running, say, combined with a program for getting strong, will be the best and fastest and most fun way to a fit and healthy body—and to feeling better than you have ever felt in your life.

4

GETTING STARTED

How Strong Are You? How Strong Do You Need to Be?

The two simple questions above do not necessarily have simple answers. Each woman differs in her basic body build, levels of skill, type of previous training, and other physiological and psychological factors. A very competitive woman with athletic talent may find it easy to win at many sports, yet her muscular strength may be no greater than that of an equally well trained partner who lacks her desire to win.

Still, how can you tell how strong *you* are? If your experience is anything like mine, you have been taking tests of various sorts throughout your life. In physical education courses you were undoubtedly tested to see how far you could throw, jump, and run. When I took those physical tests I invariably placed very low on the scale and usually took my score as some sort of personal failure. Yet I still had no idea of how strong *I* was—I only knew I was in much worse shape than most of the other kids.

This is a basic problem with most such tests: they measure you against a standard arrived at by comparing large numbers of people of varying abilities and experience. In a large sample of women, we can determine that the very best can, say, run twenty-five miles with a heavy pack on her back, while the least fit can barely walk two blocks without fatigue. In between are women of all levels, but even if you place in the fiftieth percentile in throwing ability, it does not necessarily follow that you should work hard until you can place in the top ten percent. Perhaps you just aren't built to be a great thrower or you have no reason to want to be able to throw well. The most important thing about any aspect of fitness is that it should be the best you can achieve for your own needs and within your own capabilities.

To get an exact measure of your strength (as compared to that of other women) you would have to go to a specially equipped gym or testing laboratory, where you would be put through a battery of tests administered by a specialist. If you want a *rough* idea of your present strength, though, try the following two tests at home:

Aluminum can test. This test is simple: take an empty aluminum soda can and crush it in your hand. You should be able to do so easily; if you can't, you are seriously lacking in grip strength, which correlates closely with general body strength. If this test was easy for you, move on to:

Pushup test. For this test, you will perform (or try to perform) men's pushups. First, lie down on the floor on your stomach with your palms on the floor at shoulder level, elbows pointing up in the air. Now, keeping your body straight, push yourself up with your arms until your body weight is resting only on your hands and bent toes (see illustration, p. 69). If you are like the vast majority of American women, you cannot do even one of these pushups, which are often used as a measure of upper-body strength. In the YMCA *Physical Fitness Handbook*, it is suggested that women should be able to do four to six of these (and men should be able to do eight to ten). If you can do even one of the two full pushups, you are probably much stronger than most American women.

Even without these tests, you probably have a good idea of how strong you are—which is not strong enough. But how strong *should* you be?

Dr. James Peterson of West Point feels that the amount of muscular strength a woman needs is "enough to meet the demands of her desired life-style." So, the strength requirements of a woman will vary greatly depending on whether she is a lawyer, a housewife, or an army officer (or all three).

To determine your own strength goals, ask yourself what parts of your life are made more difficult by your own lack of muscular fitness. Is it your poor golf swing, an aching back, difficulty in carrying suitcases? If you have problems in one of these areas and you intend to continue to perform the activity, then you are not strong enough to meet the demands of your own desired life-style; once the activities become easier, you are strong enough. In my own case, I felt that I was as strong as I needed to be when the problems that led me to seek upper-body strength were no longer problems: I no longer have trouble carrying my typewriter, and my paddle-ball game has improved. I have continued to work on building strength, though, both because I like the results and because I want to have a reserve of endurance to meet emergencies.

Though most women can at least function on a day-to-day basis, albeit with varying degrees of difficulty, in terms of emergency reserve most of us are very limited. An elderly lady of my acquaintance is a good example of the consequences of this lack. Sedentary from the time she was a young woman, she had not developed much upper-body strength or endurance.

One day, when she was in her seventies, she slipped and broke her hip. After convalescing, she was enrolled in a physical-therapy program to strengthen the leg muscles so that she would be able to walk again. Her therapy involved progressive workouts of the legs while she supported herself on parallel walking bars. Unfortunately, her arm strength was so poor that she couldn't support her body long enough to exercise her legs, and she had to discontinue therapy. As a result, she will probably be confined to a wheelchair for the rest of her life.

While you will probably never need to depend on your upper-body strength in such a dramatic way, the more fit you are, the better you will be able to cope with any unexpected situation or physical stress. So, in answer to the question, "How strong do I need to be?" the answer should be, "Strong enough to do the things I usually do and strong enough to handle emergencies."

Because no two women start from the same level of fitness or progress at exactly the same rate, the best way for you to measure your progress in strength building is to compare yourself with yourself. Keep a record of the exercises you are able to do at the beginning of the program, and note your progress as you continue. If you wish you can, at given intervals (say, about once a month), check to see how many more pushups you can do than you were able to do at the start of the program.

Exercising: What to Wear, Where and When

For some reason, everyone I know is worried about what to wear when exercising. The answer, of course, is dictated by common sense: wear something comfortable, something that doesn't bind at the arms, waist, or crotch. A leotard is excellent, and so are a pair of shorts and a T-shirt. When I work out, I generally wear nothing but a pair of panties. For one thing, the effort always makes me sweat, and for another I like to exercise in front of a mirror. It's somehow exciting to see my muscles actually moving while I'm working out, and seeing what I'm doing also helps me to perform the exercises correctly. For similar reasons, but with more modesty, a friend of mine works out in a bikini.

Though people who work out with very heavy weights should wear good shoes to support their feet, it's not really necessary for this program; you will probably be more comfortable barefoot or in sneakers, but again, wear whatever is most comfortable for you.

The question of where and when is easy to answer: exercise in any place that is convenient. I always work out in my bedroom/office, but you can exercise anywhere in your house; in your yard, if you have one; or in a gym. All that's really necessary is that you have enough floor space to lie down and stretch your arms all the way to the back and all the way out to the sides. If at all possible, I recommend working out in front of a full-length mirror, for the reasons I described above and also because you'll be able to see your own progress better that way.

When to exercise? Any time that is convenient for you, except just before bed or just after a meal. If you exercise at bedtime, you may find it difficult to fall asleep, because the workout will leave you feeling energetic and wide awake. And you should never engage in any strenuous activity just after eating, because when your stomach is full, a large part of your blood supply is in the intestinal tract. If you suddenly begin vigorous exercise, much of that blood supply will be diverted to your muscles, and the food can no longer be digested properly, which can result in indigestion and cramping. It's also not as easy to work out with a full stomach. If you feel you simply must have something before you exercise, try a glass of juice a few minutes before the workout, or something very easy to digest, such as yogurt. Otherwise, wait at least one hour between a meal and your workout.

If you engage in a vigorous sport or an aerobic exercise, it's generally best to do your strength workout before the exercise or sport. This is largely for the sake of motivation; I know in my own case that after my daily run, all I want to do is relax for a while, and there's no way I can get myself up for "pumping tomato juice." On the other hand, I like to work out just before running—the calisthenics and weight exercises serve as a good warmup. If you are in training for competition, though, or are about to play a very serious set of tennis, it might be best to do your workout afterward, or even skip it for that day and save your strength for the more strenuous activity.

If you are now engaged in an aerobic-exercise program, an ideal schedule would be something like the following: Monday, Wednesday, Friday—jog and do flexibility exercises; Tuesday, Thursday, Saturday—strength-building program.

Equipment

For the program in this book, there is nothing you need to buy. But after your strength improves, or if you are trying to build a lot of strength for some specific sport, you may wish to go out and purchase an inexpensive set of dumbbells.

This kind of equipment can be bought in a growing number of places: in sporting goods stores, chain department stores, and even in some health food stores. Chain stores are probably your best bet, because the equipment will cost less there. Unlike such status sports equipment as fancy warmup suits and prestige tennis rackets, a dumbbell is a dumbbell is a dumbbell, and it doesn't matter whether you get it in a posh place or at the five-and-ten. Unlike other kinds of sports equipment, dumbbells never wear out. One purchase will last you a lifetime, and how many other things can that be said of? Furthermore, dumbbells are small and can be put away easily: I simply store mine under my bed.

There are two kinds of dumbbells: cast iron and vinyl-covered cement. The vinyl equipment is cheaper than the cast iron, but if it is dropped, it can crack. Cast iron will never wear out—the only thing that might ever mar it is a little rust.

What size dumbbells should you buy? It depends on how strong you want to become. *The West Point Guide to Fitness*, which has an excellent section on weight training, recommends that for most women three sets of dumbbells are sufficient: three, five, and ten pounds. These will range in cost from about four dollars for the lightest weights to around twelve for the heaviest. Since household objects make handy substitutes for the lighter weights, probably the only dumbbell set you really need is a ten-pound one. (On certain exercises, as you become stronger, you may find the increase from five to ten pounds too much; in this case homemade substitute weights of around eight pounds would be essential.)

Another possibility, especially for women who want to go beyond the basic program, is adjustable dumbbells. These consist of two bars and several plates which attach to the bars to vary the weight. The plates come in weights from as little as one and a quarter pounds each to around two and a half pounds each. If you use adjustable dumbbells, make sure you tighten the collars that hold the plates on the bar with a wrench so they will not slip off while you are exercising; also bear in mind that the use of adjustable dumbbells may lengthen the time required for your workout, because you will have to readjust the plates from exercise to exercise. Adjustable dumbbells can bet set at up to fifty pounds and cost between twenty and thirty dollars at sporting goods and department stores.

Since dumbbells of any sort have a very small area to grip, it is important to keep your nails short so you won't dig holes in your palms while performing lifts.

An alternative to buying weights, of course, is to join a gym or health club. These have weight rooms and, in some cases, sophisticated isokinetic-exercise machines. If you simply want to find out whether you like working with weights, visit a local Y or gym— most such institutions offer trial memberships or one-time visits. If you join a gym or Y, though, I recommend checking to make sure that it also has a track or running machine, or a swimming pool or exercise bicycles so that you can get aerobic exercise too. Y's are almost always cheaper than health clubs.

The final piece of equipment you need is an exercise mat. I have a vinyl-covered foldable mat from Sears, which cost around twelve dollars. But you can easily make your own: simply place two folded blankets on the floor. Or line an old blanket with old towels, then sew it up, cross-stitching in a few places so the towels won't bunch up, and voilà: an instant exercise mat! Finally, a carpeting remnant, if you can find one large enough, would be ideal.

Homemade Weights

The suggestions below are only suggestions; you may have something around the house which works just as well or better. The only caution is that whatever you use, except for exercises requiring only one weight, you will need two of them alike: they should be the same in shape as well as in weight.

One pound. This is the very lightest weight you should use; for many women it will be too light for any of the exercises. The best one-pound weight is a can of vegetables or fruit. Though it's difficult in these days of competitive packaging to find a can that weighs exactly one pound, anything close is fine: fourteen and three-quarters, fifteen, sixteen and one-half ounces are all close enough, as long as you have two cans that weigh the same.

Two pounds. One quart of water in a plastic orange juice or detergent bottle weighs just over two pounds. A large (thirty-five ounce) can of imported tomatoes is also just over two pounds, though the cans may be difficult to manipulate if you have very small hands. Experiment to see what's easiest for you to hold.

Three pounds. For this weight I use a large can of tomato juice (one quart, fourteen ounces), which weighs just ovor three pounds. However, I have larger hands than average; if you find the cans too hard to manipulate, use your electric iron and borrow another one from a neighbor: wind the cord around the body of the iron and use the handle as a grip. Irons are even easier to hold than dumbbells.

Four to five pounds. A two-quart plastic bottle full of water weighs between four and five pounds (depending on how thick the plastic is). I have found that the easiest of these to hold are the "sculptured" types that have a very large handle extending most of the way down the side of the bottle: many laundry products come in these bottles.

Six to seven pounds. A three-quart plastic bottle (the kind fabric softener comes in) full of water weighs about two pounds more than a two-quart bottle. Again, look for the kind with a "sculptured" handle.

Heavier weights. One gallon of water in a plastic jug weighs eight to nine pounds. All the jugs I have tried are somewhat awkward to hold and are only suitable for exercises requiring one weight, or those in which a facing grip can be used, such as the biceps curl. If you plan to do a lot of work with weights of this size or heavier, buying a set of ten-pound dumbbells will probably be most practical, although even jugs can be manipulated once you get used to them.

There is one other weight that I use for a couple of exercises not requiring two matched weights, and that is a case of cat food, which weighs thirteen pounds. Although it may be a little wasteful to keep perfectly good cat food tied up in this manner, I have the advantage of knowing that if I ever run out of Fussy Feast in the middle of the night, I won't have to brave the city streets or listen to my cats complaining that I am starving them to death.

You probably won't want to lift cases of cat food, but you should easily be able to find many things around the house that can be used for weights. My friend Bonnie uses only a pair of gallon jugs, which she fills with varying amounts of water for varying weights, though she admits all the filling and emptying is a little time-consuming. Another woman fills a small overnight bag with books for the triceps exercise. Just use your imagination.

Other equipment. The only other equipment needed for this program is a broomstick or a mop handle without the cleaning implement attached.

Who Shouldn't Lift Weights

To be on the safe side, anyone should check with her doctor before beginning an exercise program, to make sure there is no condition which would make exercise inadvisable. While almost any woman can improve her own strength through this program, the older and more out of shape or overweight you are, the more slowly you should begin. Also, there are some people who should not begin any sort of conditioning program without a doctor's supervision. Do not begin the program if you have heart disease, a hernia, high blood pressure, a current infection, or a fever. Others who should be especially cautious include pregnant women and those who have had recent surgery; if you have had any surgery in the last six months, be sure to ask your doctor's advice before starting the program.

How to Exercise

As you will see, the strength-building program is a mixture of calisthenic and weight-training exercises. The following tips apply to all the exercises, whether or not they involve weights.

1. Warm up. Before you start any workout, always spend a few minutes in light preliminary activity. There are several suggested warmups in the next chapter.

2. Start slowly. The older or more out of condition

you are, the more slowly you should start. If you find it difficult to begin with the suggested starting weight, then use a lighter weight until you have increased your strength. Older women especially may find it easier to begin with the remedial exercises and gradually progress to the basic exercises for each muscle group.

3. Let work be followed by rest. Short, frequent rest pauses during the workout will give your blood a chance to rinse waste products out of your muscles, while delivering a fresh oxygen supply. If you rest up to a minute between exercises, you will be able to do even more work than if you had proceeded with the next exercise right away.

4. Exercise three times a week, but not two days in a row. Many body builders and weight lifters train every day, but they do this as a rule by exercising different muscle groups each day so that the muscles not being exercised can rest for about forty-eight hours between workouts. This is because the overload of training breaks down muscle tissue; your body needs time to rebuild this tissue (and build it stronger, to meet the new demands being made on it). I generally work out twice during the week and once on the weekend, but find the schedule that is best for you. And if you miss a workout, don't worry about it. You're not going to start losing all the strength you have gained right away—so long as you get back to the program within a day or two, you shouldn't lose any ground. On the other hand, if you skip too many sessions, your progress will be considerably slower.

One last point: if at all possible, try to schedule your workouts for the same time of day. That way, your body and mind will get used to working out at a regular time of day. This makes it easier to stick with the program.

How to Lift Weights

There are certain principles that apply to lifting weights of any size, and for best results it's necessary to follow them closely. I suggest that you read this section through now, and then when you start the program detailed in the next chapter, refer back to these pages if you have any questions.

The first and most important thing to bear in mind if you want to increase your own strength is the principle of progressive resistance, as explained in the last chapter. In order for your muscles to become stronger, they must be systematically challenged. To provide progressive resistance, you must regularly increase either the amount of weight you lift, the number of times you lift it, or both.

To keep track of these increases, there are two terms used in weight training: *repetitions* (reps) and *sets*. Repetitions, not surprisingly, are the number of times you lift a given weight or perform a given calisthenic exercise. If you lift a five-pound weight eight times, then you have just done one set of eight reps. Most weight-lifting exercises are performed in multiple sets of from one to twelve reps each, depending on the exercise, the amount of weight involved, and the particular program you are following.

There is some controversy about what particular combination of sets, reps, and weight produces the best results. The various theories are especially important for serious weight lifters who want to maximize their strength. Most experts today agree that strength is most efficiently increased by lifting a great deal of weight a few times, while endurance is improved by lifting a lesser amount of weight more times. The consensus seems to be that for optimal increase in both strength and endurance, the athlete should lift the maximum amount of weight she can handle for eight reps, in three sets, three times a week.

For our purposes, two consecutive sets of eight to twelve reps each is all that will be necessary for most exercises for the upper body (the lower-body muscle groups require more reps). Since most of us are starting from very little strength and/or endurance, this basic program will be sufficient to increase both, though once you have become stronger, and especially if you want to greatly increase a muscle group for specific sports, you may wish to experiment later on with other combinations of reps and sets.

As a rule of thumb, assume that if you can do fewer than six reps with a given weight, that weight is too heavy for you for that particular exercise; if you can easily do more than twelve, the weight is too light (though beginners will show increases in strength even when performing multiple sets of twelve reps each). Remember also that you will probably require weights of different sizes for different exercises.

The idea of continually increasing resistance is a particularly difficult one for most women, because we are not used to challenging ourselves physically. I know that when I began the program, before certain exercises I would think, "I just can't face this one more time!" But then I would add one more rep, straining to do so, and by the next session I usually found that one rep further or even a heavier weight was now necessary to provide a challenge.

A friend of mine who went through the program with me couldn't understand why she wasn't getting the same results I was. It became clear when I watched her exercise one day. While the exercises were far easier for her to do than they had been at the beginning, she had not changed the amount of weight she was using, and had increased her reps by only a few. When I asked her why she had not progressed beyond three-pound weights, she replied, "Well, it's *hard.*"

Exactly. Every workout should be hard. Not to the point of excruciating pain, but hard enough to let you know you have worked out. You'll know this because you will sweat, your heart will pound, and your muscles will feel tired when you have finished. If this isn't happening, you are not challenging your muscles sufficiently and you will not increase your strength.

Always keep in mind the idea of *progressive* overloading; add more weight in small increments to build strength and add reps in small increments to build endurance.

Grips

The way you hold the weight is very important in some of the exercises, and it can affect the results. We will be using two basic grips, overhand and underhand, as well as a modified grip, with hands facing each other (see illustrations 1a, 1b, 1c, p. 55).

The overhand grip is just what it sounds like: you hold the weight with your hand *over* it. The underhand grip is the opposite: you grasp the weight from beneath. The alternate grip is basically a variation of the overgrip, with palms facing each other.

Overhand grip   **Underhand grip**

Alternate grip

Performing Lifts

It might seem strange to have to be told how to lift a weight. It seems absurdly simple—you just grab hold of it and lift, right? Well, it *is* simple, but proper technique is crucial for best results, and these few rules, carefully followed, will assure your rapid progress.

The most important thing to remember in lifting a weight is to lift *steadily*. Don't jerk the weight—your muscles should be in complete control of it at all times. If a weight is so heavy that you can only raise it by "throwing" it upward at the beginning of the lift, that weight is too heavy for you, and you should choose a lighter one.

If a weight is to be lifted by a particular muscle, try to use *only* that muscle; for example, if the instructions for an exercise tell you to keep your back straight throughout, and you suddenly find yourself bending toward the back, other muscles are becoming involved in the exercise, and you should therefore switch to a lighter weight or a lower number of reps.

It's often tempting to cheat a little to make an exercise seem easier, but ultimately you're only cheating yourself by depriving yourself of the full benefits of the exercise. It's especially easy to "cheat" when you are lowering a weight, because gravity is on your side. For this reason it's important to concentrate on the lowering part of any lift: perform it slowly and deliberately, and make sure that it takes about the same amount of time as raising the weight did.

Finally, perform your lifts through the greatest range of motion given in the instructions for the exercise. If a weight is supposed to be extended fully over your head, bring your arms up as high as they can go on *every* rep; not only will this maximize your gains in muscular strength, it will improve your flexibility.

When you finish a set, rest about one minute, and then perform the next set.

Breathing

You may have heard that proper breathing is very important in strenuous exercise, and it is; in fact, when lifting very heavy weights, incorrect breathing can actually be dangerous. For the amount of weight you will be lifting in this program, you don't need to worry about breathing except for this one very important point: NEVER HOLD YOUR BREATH WHILE LIFTING WEIGHTS. Just breathe naturally. You may find the pacing of the exercise is easier if you raise and lower the weights in time with the rhythm of your own breath.

Finally, concentrate on what you're doing. I have found it very helpful when performing lifts to visualize in my mind what each muscle is doing while it works. When I lift a weight in my hand, I try to "see" the muscle shortening as it pulls the weight up toward my shoulder. Visualizing in this way somehow makes the exercise easier, and it also helps ensure that it will be done correctly.

What to Expect

I can't pretend that you will find the program all fun and games. Particularly at first, it may be difficult to stick with because the exercises are new and strenuous—but they quickly become easier as you gain more experience with them. On the other hand, many women find that the novelty of lifting weights is fun and much less boring than traditional programs.

One thing I can practically guarantee is that you will experience some muscle soreness, at least in the first few run-throughs of the program. (If you don't experience some soreness, you aren't challenging your muscles enough and should increase the amount of weight and/or reps that you are using.) The peak of the soreness usually comes between twelve and thirty-six hours after exercise. Surprisingly, one of the best things to do to relieve it is to perform the exercise again.

Physiologists are not sure what causes this soreness —perhaps it is a result of waste products or small tears in the muscle tissue, but one thing all experts agree on is that it becomes much less noticeable or disappears entirely after you have been on the program for a while.

Another not altogether pleasant side effect you may experience is relative weakness in your arms and hands for some time after a workout. While this is not severe enough to cause you to lose control of your hands, it may be noticeable for an hour or two. I try not to do any heavy typing after I work out, though of course I can manage it if I have to.

Another thing you can expect is occasional setbacks. Don't worry about them; all athletes in all sports suffer them. While you may have been making tremendous progress, increasing your weight and your reps with every workout, you may suddenly discover at one session that you can't lift as well as you did three sessions back. Simply accept it, and do as well as you can; you will probably find that you're able to advance again by the next session. In fact, I often find that I lift *better* on days following a particularly bad workout.

These sudden increases in strength or endurance,

alternating with sessions of no improvement, are known as the plateau effect. No one really understands just how or why this works, but in all areas of exercise and sports performance, it is common to have stale periods followed by periods of rapid gain; after the gain, a plateau is reached, and once again you may feel as if you aren't making much progress.

In general, though, and particularly at the beginning of the program, you can expect quick results. While these may not be dramatic, they will be noticeable: it's not unusual to increase your strength slightly from the first to the second exercise session. Though each woman will progress at a different rate, you should be able to see positive changes within four or five sessions—changes in the amount of weight you use in the exercises, changes in your daily life and in your appearance.

Finally, expect to feel good. In spite of the occasional aches and pains you will experience after some workouts, you will probably develop a new awareness of your body. Formerly tense areas, such as your upper back and neck, will begin to loosen up; all daily activities, from working to walking, will be easier because you will be stronger and more limber. For perhaps the first time in your life you will experience your body as a dynamic, versatile machine, with each part of it working the way it was meant to.

5

GETTING STRONG:
THE PROGRAM

Before beginning the exercises in the strength-building program, you should always spend a little time—at least five minutes—on warming up. The warmup serves two functions: it accustoms your body to an increasing level of activity and it helps you maintain flexibility. Warming up is especially important for women over the age of twenty-five—as we grow older, our tissues become less elastic and thus more subject to strain.

If you have taken a calisthenics or yoga class, you may already know some good preliminary exercises you can use to warm up. The main thing to remember is that your preliminary exercises should consist of gentle stretching—never bouncing. Bouncing can cause a rebound effect, with subsequent tightening of the very muscles you are trying to stretch.

Following are five warmups, each emphasizing a different part of your body. Choose some or all of them before each workout:

1. *Back stretcher.* Bend over from the waist, keeping your legs straight and letting your arms and head drop, and just *hang.* Don't try to force yourself any closer to the ground, and don't tighten any of your

muscles; just relax and let gravity do its work of unkinking your back and stretching the muscles of your back and legs. Hold for one minute. Repeat two or three times.

2. *Arm stretcher.* Stand with your feet comfortably apart, your hands and arms straight overhead. Reach upward, slowly, as high as possible with one hand, as if you were trying to touch the ceiling. Hold at the extreme position for a few seconds, then reach slowly with the other hand. Repeat several times with each hand.

3. *Side stretcher.* Stand with your feet comfortably apart, your right hand on your waist, your left arm overhead. Now gently bend to the right side until you feel a stretching on your left side. Hold for a few seconds, then reverse the positions of your hands and bend to the other side. Repeat several times on each side.

4. *Calf stretcher.* Stand about two feet from a wall, facing it. Stretch out your arms and lean against the wall, supporting yourself with your hands. Keep your feet flat on the floor as you lean into the wall, hold ten seconds, then push yourself away from the wall, as if you were doing a pushup against it. You should feel a stretching in your calf muscles; if you don't, move your feet farther from the wall. Repeat two or three times.

This exercise is an especially important warmup for women, because so many of us have shortened calf muscles caused by years of wearing high-heeled shoes.

5. *Half-forward bend.* Sit on the floor with your legs stretched out in front of you. With your right leg straight and keeping both legs on the floor, bend your left leg and bring your left foot as close to your body as possible (it should rest just at your crotch). Now, without bending your right knee, reach forward

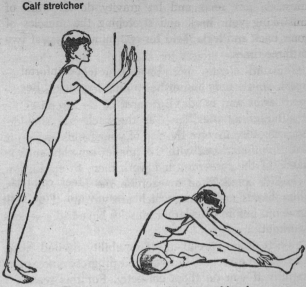

Calf stretcher

Half-forward bend

with both hands and grasp your right leg, ankle, or foot, as far down as you can reach without straining. Ideally, your body should rest along the length of the leg, your head on your knee, and your fingers grasping your toes, but don't push for this extreme position— go only as far as is comfortable. Hold for thirty seconds, relaxing consciously. Reverse the position and repeat with your other leg. This exercise will help loosen tight leg muscles and is also good for stretching your back.

Basic Strength Program for Women

The program on the following pages consists of nine exercises, each for a different muscle group of your body. You must do all nine exercises; that is, one from each muscle group. With one exception, it's important to do the exercises in the order given, particularly the exercises for the upper body. Common sense and a little thought explain why: if you are weak in all your upper-body muscles, that includes your arms and hands. But most of the exercises for the larger muscles, such as the back and shoulder muscles, also involve the use of your hands and arms. So, if you start out with the smaller muscles, such as those of the forearms, and work them to exhaustion, when it comes time to exercise the larger muscles, your hands and arms, which are already tired, will give out before your larger muscles have had a serious workout.

There is no special talent or ability needed to do any of the exercises, but you will progress much more rapidly if you do them correctly. For this reason, I suggest that you go through the program at least once without any weights at all, just performing the motions and watching yourself in a mirror. Then, when you start working with weights, you will be familiar with the way to manipulate them.

As for choosing a weight to begin with, you will have to experiment to see what works for you. In general, it will be a weight that you can lift, but with some difficulty, six to eight times for two consecutive sets. By "some difficulty" I mean that the weight should feel heavy for the first few reps, and should require you to exert considerable force for the last couple of reps. (The amount of weight you use will vary from exercise to exercise.) For each exercise I will give a recommended starting weight and a suggested goal. The goals are only recommendations, of course—once you reach the basic goal (for most women this will be in about ten weeks), you can stop there and just maintain your strength, or you can continue to increase your reps and weights. (See Chapter Six.) The only limit to the amount of strength you can develop is the amount of time and effort you want to put in.

There are four variations given for most of the nine exercises. These are:

Exercise A—Easy. These are really remedial exercises, and you should choose an A exercise only if you find it impossible to perform B or C for that muscle group. Some women will need to do A for a while on one or more exercises; others won't need to do A at all. If you start with an A exercise, move on to a B or a C as soon as you can.

Exercise B—Basic. This is the basic strength-building exercise for each muscle group covered in the program, and in most cases B makes use of weights.

Exercise C—Alternate. Whenever possible, I have provided an alternate exercise which does *not* make use of weights (though for some muscle groups weights are essential). C exercises are for the most part traditional calisthenics, and the weight of your own body provides the resistance for your muscles to work against. Feel free to switch back and forth between the B and C exercises as you move through the program, but be aware that it may slow your progress.

Exercise D—Advanced. Move on to a D exercise when B or C becomes too easy, or if you wish to go beyond the basic goals of the program.

Supplemental and substitute exercises will be provided in the next chapter. Following is a detailed description of the exercises to be performed on the program. At the end of this section is a summary chart for easy reference.

GROUP I: LEGS

By far the best exercises for strengthening your legs are running, walking, and bicycling. If you are now engaged in an aerobics program of running, walking, or biking, your legs are probably already strong, and you needn't do the exercises for this muscle group unless you want to (just walking to the corner store a couple of times a week doesn't count, however).

A. Easy. WALK CONTINUOUSLY FOF FIFTEEN MINUTES

B. Basic. BENCH STEP

Start: Stand in front of a sturdy bench or chair.
Move: Put your right foot on the chair; then step up onto the chair with your left foot. Immediately lower your right foot to the floor, then your left. Repeat this

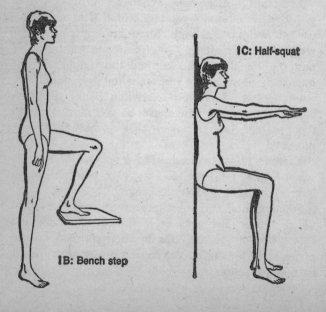

1C: Half-squat

1B: Bench step

sequence for one minute; then switch the lead to your left foot and repeat.

Goal: Start with two minutes (one minute with each foot in the lead), then build to ten minutes.

Comment: You may find that this exercise causes pain in your calf muscles; this is normal and nothing to worry about. Because it is somewhat strenuous, this exercise should not be performed without your doctor's advice if you are middle-aged, are very much overweight, or have a heart condition. On the bright side, the bench step can also be used as an aerobic conditioning program.

C. *Alternate.* HALF-SQUAT

Start: Stand leaning with your back against a wall, feet comfortably apart and twelve to fifteen inches from the wall, your arms stretched out in front of you for balance.

Move: Using the wall as a support and keeping your back straight, slide down until you are sitting on air, thighs parallel with the floor. Slowly rise to a standing position. Repeat.

Goal: Start with eight repetitions; build to twenty.

D. *Advanced.* PERFORM B HOLDING WEIGHTS IN YOUR HANDS, YOUR ARMS AT YOUR SIDES. INCREASE THE PACE AND NUMBER OF REPETITIONS

GROUP II: CHEST AND FRONT OF SHOULDERS

A. *Easy.* ARM LIFTS

Start: Lie on your back, with your arms on the floor, straight out to the sides. Your open palms should be facing the ceiling.

Move: Slowly bring your arms straight up off the floor, toward each other, until your hands almost meet in the air above your chest. Slowly lower.

Reps: Start with eight repetitions of this exercise. build to twenty.

Goal: Twenty to thirty repetitions, until you can perform this exercise with a weight (however light) in each hand.

B. *Basic.* ARM LIFTS WITH WEIGHTS

Start: Lie as for A, but hold a weight in each hand in an underhand grip (your palms facing the ceiling).

Move: Slowly bring your arms straight up, as in A. Pause briefly, then slowly lower the weights to starting position.

Suggested starting weight: Three pounds. Start with two consecutive sets of six to eight reps each. Build to two sets of twelve reps, then go on to a heavier weight at two sets of six to eight reps.

Goal: Two sets of twelve reps with a weight of eight to ten pounds per hand.

Comment: Since this exercise strengthens and tones your pectorals, you may find after you have performed it for a while that your breasts appear firmer and higher.

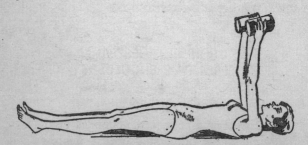

II B: Arm lifts with weights

C. *Alternate*. PUSHING

The pushup is one of the best overall exercises for your upper body: to some extent, it involves all of the upper-body muscle groups. Because pushups are such a comprehensive exercise, they are suggested as the C exercise for three of the muscle groups (besides this group, the shoulders and triceps). I urge you to do pushups as a frequent alternate to the B exercise, but do not substitute them for more than one muscle group in any given workout.

You may choose from two types of pushup: the negative pushup and the modified pushup.

Negative Pushup

This is simply the lowering part of a standard men's pushup. It's an excellent exercise for women for two reasons. First, most women can't do full men's pushups. But a muscle is capable of lowering a great deal more weight than it can raise (when it is working against gravity). So the negative pushup is a good way for women with weak muscles to get many benefits of the full pushup while at the same time gradually strengthening the muscles used in that exercise.

Start: Begin in the upper part of a man's standard pushup—palms directly below shoulders, fingers

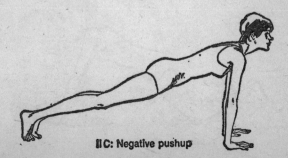

II C: Negative pushup

pointing ahead, arms straight, back straight. Your body is off the floor. All weight should be on your palms and bent toes.

Move: Slowly lower yourself to the floor, *keeping your trunk straight.* Return to starting position without trying to perform the other part of the pushup. Simply scramble up; how you return to the start is irrelevant in this exercise. All that is important is the slow, straight lowering of your body.

Goal: Start with as many as you can do. For most women this will probably be two to five reps at first. Build to twenty reps.

Modified Pushup

Start: Keeping your back straight, support yourself on your knees and outstretched palms. Your arms should be straight, your hands resting on the floor in front of you, shoulder-width apart. Your body is at an angle to the floor.

Move: Slowly lower your upper body to the ground, keeping your trunk straight and your elbows pointing straight up. Now raise yourself back to starting position.

Goal: Start with as many as you can do; build to twenty.

II C: Modified pushup

D. Advanced. ADD MORE WEIGHT TO B OR DO FULL MEN'S PUSHUPS

Start: Assume the same position as for the negative pushup.

Move: Lower your body to the ground, as in the negative pushup, but when your chest touches the floor, straighten your arms and raise your body back to the starting position. Repeat.

Goal: Start with as many as you can do (this may be as few as one) and build to sixteen repetitions.

Comment: The most difficult part of this exercise (once your arms are strong enough to support your body weight) is keeping your trunk straight while raising the body. If you cannot do this correctly, it is better to continue to build strength through a less strenuous exercise.

GROUP III: UPPER BACK

A. Easy. ARM FLINGS

Start: Stand, feet comfortably apart, arms out at shoulder level. Bend your elbows until your fingers touch in front of your chest.

Move: First, fling your bent elbows as far back as possible. (Try to make them meet in the back.) Return to start. Now, straighten your arms and fling them as far back as possible, keeping them parallel to the floor. Return to starting position. Repeat, alternately flinging bent and straight arms.

Goal: Start with ten reps of each fling. Build to twenty each.

B. Basic. LYING OVERHEAD LIFTS

Start: Lie on your back with your arms at your sides, a weight held in each hand in an overhand grip

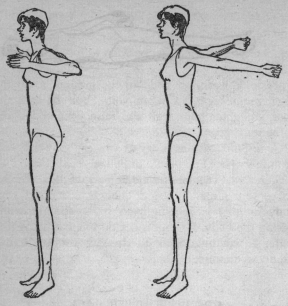

III A: Arm flings (views 1 and 2)

(your palms facing the floor). You may bend your knees if you find it more comfortable.

Move: Bring your arms straight up in the air, then over your head and straight back to the floor behind you. As the weight just touches the floor, pause, then lift your arms straight up again and slowly lower them to starting position.

Suggested starting weight: One to two pounds. Start with two consecutive sets of six to eight reps each. Build to two sets of twelve reps, then go on to a heavier weight at two sets of six.

Goal: Two sets of twelve reps with a weight of five pounds.

Comment: Most women find this exercise extremely difficult to perform at first, though improvement is

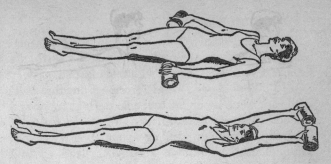

fll B: Lying overhead lifts (views 1 and 2)

usually very rapid. If performing this exercise with a weight in each hand is too hard for you, you may find it easier if you hold one weight in both hands, or you may begin the exercise with your arms straight overhead (as in the bench press, p. 96). For a greater range of motion, as well as a stretching of the diaphragm area, try doing this lift with two or three large pillows under the *small* of your back (your hips should slant down, as should your upper body).

C. Alternate. SWIM FOR FIFTEEN MINUTES (THE CRAWL STROKE)

D. Advanced. ADD MORE WEIGHT TO B

GROUP IV: LOWER BACK

Lower-back pain can result from many causes, only some of which have to do with the strength of the lower back itself. Weak abdominal muscles and too-tight hamstrings are among the leading contributors to this malady. If you do have lower-back pain, be sure to check with your doctor before performing exercises for this group; in any case, do them slowly and easily to avoid injury.

A. Easy. FORWARD BEND

Start: Stand comfortably, with your hands clasped behind your neck, your elbows straight out to the sides, and your legs straight, with feet together.

Move: Very slowly, bend forward from the waist until your trunk is parallel to the floor. Hold for several seconds, then slowly return upright. Try to feel your lower-back muscles pulling your body upright. Throughout this exercise, keep your head up and your back straight.

Goal: Start with three to five repetitions; build to sixteen.

B. Basic. FORWARD BEND WITH WEIGHT

Start: Stand as for A, except instead of clasping hands behind your neck, hold a weight behind your neck with both hands, palms facing inward.

Move: Keeping the weight stationary behind your head, bend slowly forward from the waist until your trunk is parallel to the ground. Hold for several sec-

IV B: Forward bend with weight

onds, then slowly return upright. Keep your head up and your back straight.

Suggested starting weight: Five pounds. Start with one set of six to eight reps, build to twenty, then go on to a heavier weight at six reps.

Goal: Twenty reps with a weight of ten pounds.

Comment: One advantage of this exercise is that since you aren't actually manipulating a weight, the weight doesn't have to be easy to hold. I use my thirteen-pound cat-food box for this one, but you could use almost anything that provides a little challenge. *Don't* use a weight of more than ten to fifteen pounds for this exercise; to further improve strength in the lower back it is better and safer to increase the number of reps than the amount of weight used.

C. *Alternate.* BACK LEG RAISES

Start: Lie on your stomach, with your head resting comfortably on your folded hands, and a folded pillow tucked underneath your abdomen and groin.

Move: Slowly lift your left leg straight up as far as you can, hold for seven to ten seconds, then slowly lower it. Repeat with the right leg.

Goal: Twelve lifts with each leg, *not* alternately. Start with three to five each.

D. *Advanced.* ADD MORE REPS TO B

IV C: Back leg raises

GROUP V: SHOULDERS

A. *Easy.* SIDE ARM LIFTS

Start: Stand with your feet comfortably apart, your arms at your sides.

Move: Keeping your arms straight, bring them slowly out at the sides and up until your hands are over your head. Slowly lower to starting position.

Goal: The goal of this exercise is to lift your arms while holding weights. Start with eight reps; build to twenty or more, until you can comfortably move on to B.

B. *Basic.* SIDE ARM LIFTS WITH WEIGHTS

Start: Stand with your feet comfortably apart, arms at your sides, a weight in each hand held in an over-hand grip (your palms facing your sides, your knuckles facing the floor).

Move: Keep your legs straight and your *trunk bent slightly forward* as you raise your arms out to the sides and up until they are straight overhead. Hold a moment, then slowly lower.

Suggested starting weight: Two to three pounds. Start with two consecutive sets of six to eight reps each, build to two sets of twelve reps, then go on to a heavier weight at two sets of six to eight reps.

Goal: Two sets of twelve reps with a weight of five pounds.

Comment: This exercise is somewhat difficult for most women. If you find it very easy, check to make sure that your trunk is bent *slightly* forward from the waist. It's easy to lift even fairly heavy weights part-way up, but the key to this lift is getting the arms up there above shoulder level.

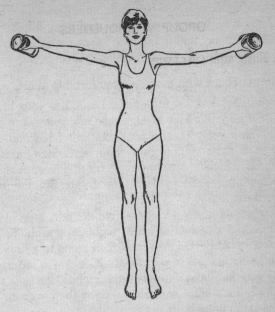

VB: Side arm lifts with weights

C. Alternate. PUSHUPS (SEE II C)

D. Advanced. ADD MORE WEIGHT TO B OR DO FULL
PUSHUPS

GROUP VI: FRONTS OF UPPER ARMS

There is one best exercise for developing the fronts
of your upper arms: the biceps curl.

A, B, and C. BICEPS CURL

Start: Stand comfortably with your arms at your
sides, a weight in each hand. If you are using dumbbells or a lightweight can, hold the weight in an

underhand grip, palms facing the front, knuckles facing the floor. If you are using a plastic jug filled with water, you may find it easier to use the alternate grip: grasp the jugs by their handles, palms facing each other.

Move: Slowly raise your right forearm, keeping your elbows back and held to your sides. When your hand has reached shoulder level, pause momentarily, then begin to lower your arm back to starting position. *At the same time,* start to raise your left arm. Continue alternately raising and lowering; try to concentrate on the lowering, keeping both arms in steady and controlled motion.

Suggested starting weight: Five pounds. Start with two consecutive sets of six to eight reps each. Build to two sets of twelve reps each, then go on to a heavier weight at two sets of six to eight. Count one rep each time your left hand returns to starting position.

Goal: Two sets of twelve reps with a weight of eight to ten pounds.

Comment: This exercise involves other muscles besides your biceps. If you are lifting too heavy a weight, these muscles will come into play in an obvious way. Toward the end of a set of reps, guard against the tendency to bend backwards as one arm reaches the top of its motion; your back should be held straight and steady throughout. When you arch your back you are cheating, in that much of the stress of the lift is taken away from the biceps.

GROUP VII: BACKS OF UPPER ARMS

A. *Easy.* WALL PUSHUP

Start: Stand one to two feet from a wall, with your arms straight out in front of you and your hands supporting you as you lean into the wall.

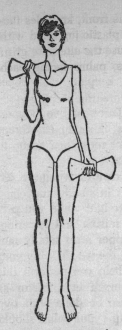

VI A, B, C: Biceps curl

VII B: Triceps press

Move: Slowly lower your body to the wall, then push it back out.

Goal: Start with eight reps; build to sixteen.

Comment: This exercise is similar to the calf stretcher (see p. 62), but here the emphasis is on pushing the weight of your body away from the wall as you straighten your elbows.

B. *Basic.* TRICEPS PRESS

Start: Stand with your feet comfortably apart and your arms straight overhead, your hands holding one weight, your palms facing each other.

Move: Slowly bend your elbows, keeping them close to your head, lowering the weight until it just touches the upper part of your back. Your upper arms should not move backward; they should cover your ears, and your elbows should be pointing straight up in the air. Hold this position for three to five seconds, then slowly raise the weight, keeping your upper arms motionless.

Suggested starting weight: Three to five pounds. Start with two consecutive sets of six to eight reps each. Build to two sets of twelve reps, then go on to a heavier weight at two sets of six.

Goal: Two sets of twelve reps with a weight of ten pounds.

Comment: Keep your back straight while you perform this exercise. Also, while raising and lowering, concentrate on keeping your upper arms totally motionless. In raising and lowering the weight, only your forearms should move. It may help you perform this exercise correctly to watch yourself in a mirror as you work. This exercise can also be done with two weights held in an overhand grip (your palms should be facing each other).

C. Alternate. PUSHUPS (SEE II C)

D. Advanced. ADD MORE WEIGHT TO B OR DO FULL MEN'S PUSHUPS

GROUP VIII: FOREARMS, WRISTS, HANDS

A. Easy. WRIST ROLLER

Start: Stand with your legs comfortably apart, elbows bent and forearms straight out in front at waist level. Hold a broomstick in an overhand grip (your palms facing the floor), your hands separated by a few inches.

Move: Rotate the broom handle as though you

were rolling up a map. Keep your hands completely closed around the broomstick.

Goal: Perform this exercise until your hands and forearms feel fatigued. For most women, twenty to thirty reps (a rep counts as each time you move your right hand) will be enough to start with; build to forty reps.

B. Basic. WRIST ROLLER WITH WEIGHT

Start: This is performed exactly as in A, except that a weight is attached to the center of the broomstick by a string long enough to reach the floor. To keep the string from slipping, you may want to pound a tack into the broomstick and attach the string to it. Wrapping several layers of adhesive or electrician's

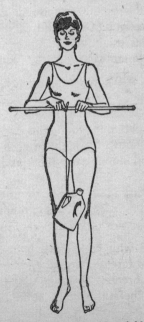

VIII B: Wrist roller with weight

tape around the broom where the string attaches also helps prevent slipping.

Move: Same as in A, except that the goal is to wind the string around the handle until the weight reaches the handle. Then unwind the string and start over for a second set.

Suggested starting weight: One to three pounds. Start with one set and work up to four sets; then go on to a heavier weight and one set.

Goal: Four sets with a weight of eight to ten pounds.

Comment: For me and several friends on the program, this was the most difficult exercise to perform, but improvement was especially rapid. This exercise also involves your upper-arm (and other) muscles. Because it may be more difficult to perform right after you have exercised your upper arms, you may switch the order of the exercise in this group with that in the last group (Group IX).

C. Alternate. WRIST CURLS

Start: Sit or stand at a table, bench, desk, or anything that supports your forearms while allowing your hands and wrists to hang off the edge.

Move: For part one, your arms and palms should be facing up. Grasp a weight in each hand (underhand grip) and slowly raise them as far as possible,

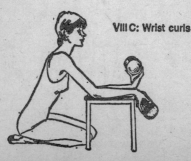

VIII C: Wrist curls

while keeping your forearms on the table. Slowly lower the weights, then repeat. For part two, your arms and palms should be facing down. Grasp the weight in an overhand grip and proceed as for part one.

Suggested starting weight: Three pounds. Start with two consecutive sets of six to eight reps each; build to two sets of twelve reps, then go on to a heavier weight at two sets of six to eight.

D. *Advanced.* ADD MORE WEIGHT TO EITHER B OR C

GROUP IX: ABDOMEN

Situps and leg raises, when properly performed, are the best exercises for building abdominal strength. There are many different types of situps, though most are just variations on a basic theme. You may have heard that straight-legged situps are the "best" kind and that they are a goal you should aim for; indeed, many exercise books and programs still recommend straight-legged situps. The trouble with these is that they involve other, stronger, muscle groups, particularly the front hip muscles. This is fine and dandy if you have strong abdominal muscles to begin with, but if your abdominals are weak, the hip muscles will simply take over more of the work of performing the situp, and your abdominals won't get much of a workout.

To overcome this problem, most experts now recommend some variation of the bent-legged situp, which involves your hip muscles to a lesser extent.

A. *Easy.* HALF-SITUP

Start: Lie on your back with your knees bent, your arms at your sides.

IX B: Chair situp

Move: Keeping your chin tucked into your chest, slowly curl up until your head, shoulders, chest, and arms are just off the floor; then curl back down. Repeat. Be sure to keep your lower back *flat* on the floor.

Goal: Start with six to eight reps; build to twenty-five.

B. *Basic.* CHAIR SITUP

Start: Lie on your back with your knees bent and your lower legs resting on the seat of a chair. Your lower back should be *flat* on the floor. If possible, hook your feet under the chair back. A bridge chair is ideal for this, but you can use anything of the right height. Your arms should be folded across your chest, your chin tucked into your chest.

Move: Curl slowly up off the floor until you are nearly sitting; slowly uncurl, trying to feel your back unroll vertebra by vertebra.

Goal: Start with six to eight reps; work up to twenty-five.

C. *Alternate.* BENT-LEGGED SITUP

Same as A, except that your hands should be clasped behind your head, and you should try to come all the way up. As in B, when you return to the starting posi-

IX C: Bent-legged situp

tion, try to feel your back unwind slowly, vertebra by vertebra.

D. Advanced. HOLD A WEIGHT OF UP TO FIVE POUNDS JUST UNDER YOUR CHIN WITH BOTH HANDS, THEN PROCEED AS FOR B

Comment: The position of your hands makes a difference in the difficulty of the exercise. The easiest position is with your arms folded across your chest; the hardest, with your hands behind your head. If you find the latter too hard, try the hands-in-front position; as it becomes easier, you can use the hands-behind-head position.

On the next page is a chart summarizing the Basic Strength Program for Women.

Recording Your Progress

In any sort of conditioning program, it is important to keep a record of your performances. If for each exercise you note how many reps you did with how much weight, there will be no confusion when you begin your next workout. Just as important, seeing your own progress in black and white can help motivate you to keep going.

BASIC STRENGTH PROGRAM FOR WOMEN

SUMMARY CHART

EXERCISE	MUSCLE GROUP	Easy A	Basic B	Alternate C
I	LEGS	Walk 15 Minutes	Bench Step	Half-Squat
II	CHEST-FRONTS OF SHOULDERS	Arm Lifts	Arm Lifts with Wts.	Pushups
III	UPPER BACK	Arm Flings	Lying Overhead Lifts	Swim
IV	LOWER BACK	Forward Bend	Forward Bend with Wts.	Back Leg Raises
V	SHOULDERS	Side Arm Lifts	Side Arm Lifts with Wts.	Pushups
VI	FRONTS OF UPPER ARMS	Biceps Curl	Biceps Curl	Biceps Curl
VII	BACKS OF UPPER ARMS	Wall Pushup	Triceps Press	Pushups
VIII	FOREARMS	Wrist Roller	Wrist Roller with Wt.	Wrist Curls
IX	ABDOMEN	Half Situp	Chair Situp	Bent-Legged Situp

On the next two pages is a sample exercise log to take you through the first eight weeks of the program.

Of course you can keep your records any way you wish, but I have found the following shorthand notation to be helpful. For each group, I note first the exercise I am doing (usually B), then the number of reps, followed by an X (meaning times), followed by the weight I used. If I did more than one set, I write that last, circling it. Thus, B10 x 5 ② means that for this group I performed the B exercise in two sets of ten reps with a weight of five pounds.

I also write occasional comments to myself on the chart—if an exercise is particularly hard or easy one day, I note that down and bear it in mind for the next time I do the exercise.

If, in looking back over your exercise log, you discover that progress in one particular exercise is not as rapid as in the others, it might be a signal to go back and review the basic instructions for the exercise. Perhaps you are not performing it correctly, or maybe you are using the wrong weight. (On the other hand, don't expect to proceed at exactly the same rate for every exercise. Some will naturally be harder than others, depending on your previous experience.)

It will take different women different amounts of time to achieve the suggested goals for the basic program. Based on my experience and that of other women who have tried my program, you can probably expect to achieve these basic goals within eight to twelve weeks. But if your progress is faster or slower, don't worry about it. You're not in competition with anyone, so you can't lose. On the contrary, you can only gain—a stronger, shapelier, and fitter body.

BASIC STRENGTH PROGRAM FOR WOMEN

EXERCISE LOG

date	I LEGS	II CHEST FRONT SHOULDERS	III UPPER BACK	IV LOWER BACK	V SHOULDERS	VI FRONT UPPER ARMS	VII BACK UPPER ARMS	VIII FOREARMS	IX ABDOMEN
SAMPLE	4 min/bal 20 min	2B x 5 @ not too hard	2b x 2 @ very hard	120 x 8	B 10 x 3 @	2/2 x 5 @ try tomy cot	2B x 5 @ def not it	2/ x 8 agony!	88
WEEK 1 — 1									
WEEK 1 — 2									
WEEK 1 — 3									
WEEK 2 — 1									
WEEK 2 — 2									
WEEK 2 — 3									
WEEK 3 — 1									
WEEK 3 — 2									
WEEK 3 — 3									

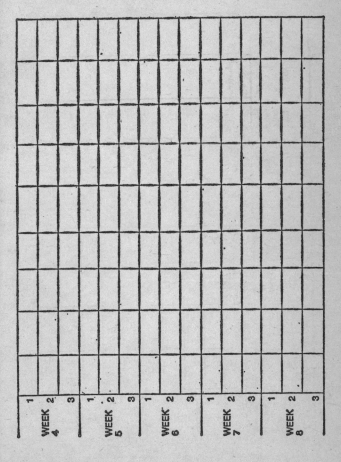

WEEK 4 1 2 3
WEEK 5 1 2 3
WEEK 6 1 2 3
WEEK 7 1 2 3
WEEK 8 1 2 3

6

STAYING STRONG

"Maintenance is easy. It's getting there that's difficult."
—Dr. Dorothy Harris, Penn State University.

So now you are strong—or at least stronger. But what now? Do you continue to increase your weights and reps indefinitely, or do you stop? And if you do stop, how can you best maintain your new-found strength?

The answers to these questions depend on you and your own needs—which may change throughout your life, requiring periodic reevaluation. What are your present needs? Do you want to become even stronger? If so, you will have to continue to increase the difficulty of your workouts. And if you do wish to go on, just how much stronger do you want to become? Following are three suggested levels of maintenance to be followed once you have completed the basic program. Read them through to decide which level is best for you.

Level I. *Minimal.* If you are satisfied with the increase in strength and changes in your body achieved through meeting the goals of the Basic Strength Program, then you can stop right here—which does not mean that you stop working out altogether, but that you stop adding reps and more weight to your exercises, and you stop exercising three times a week (unless you prefer to work out that often).

How often must you work out to maintain your strength? There's no hard-and-fast rule about this, but if you can, exercise twice a week with the number of reps and amount of weights you were using when you completed the basic program. If you occasionally skip a workout, you shouldn't notice any real loss of conditioning, as long as you continue to exercise at least once a week. But if you find any exercises becoming difficult, increase the number of times you work out, until you return to your basic level of strength.

Level 2. *Continuing.* This is for women who want to go beyond the goals of the basic program but who do not want to try heavier weights. To continue to build strength without using heavier weights, simply increase the number of sets of each exercise from two to three. (Of course, when you first increase the number of sets, you will almost certainly have to reduce the number of reps per set until your body adjusts to the increased workload.)

Just as important, now is the time to add variety to the basic program, which will keep you from getting stale, as well as exercising your muscles in new ways. Begin substituting new exercises for some of your regular exercises; you can also add supplemental exercises for muscle groups that you particularly want to work on. (For supplemental and substitute exercises, see p. 94.)

When you feel that you have attained the strength you need or want on this continuing program, you can maintain it by working out at least once—but preferably twice—a week, at the maximum levels you have achieved. And as with the minimal program, you won't lose much ground if you occasionally have to skip a workout.

Level 3. *Advanced*. Women who want to greatly increase their strength for sports or other reasons should continue to add to the amount of weight they use, as well as to increase the number of sets to three.

For the next several weeks, you can continue to follow the basic program, up to the point where home-made weights and dumbbells no longer challenge your muscles sufficiently. When that happens, it is time to buy more sophisticated equipment and/or join a gym.*

As with women on the continuing program, you will want to add substitute exercises to your basic program, as well as to work on supplemental exercises for the muscle groups you are most interested in strengthening.

Again, once you have achieved your desired level of strength, you can maintain it by working out only once or twice a week at the highest level you have achieved.

It is not necessary to use substitute exercises for each muscle group, but you will find it much easier to stick with the program if you substitute and add supplements for some muscle groups every few weeks. This is because psychologically and physically it's natural to grow tired of the same old routine. This applies to any exercise regimen: although I usually do my daily jog on a neighborhood track, occasionally I run in the park or through the streets instead. This is never by plan—I do it on days when I just feel like it. For the Basic Strength Program (after the minimal goals have been reached), you can likewise add variety whenever you feel like it.

*See section on heavy weights in Chapter Eleven: Getting Strong for Sports.

Supplemental and Substitute Exercises

The following exercises can be performed with homemade weights or with dumbbells. Remember that even though you have achieved the goals of the basic program, you may have to drop back to a lower level of both reps and weights when you first perform a new exercise.

When substituting an exercise for the first time, stay with it for at least three exercise sessions before switching back, so that you will have time to master it. (If you are on the minimal maintenance program, do not substitute an exercise without briefly—for a period of three to four weeks—returning to the basic program of working out three times a week.) A supplemental exercise (E) should not be substituted for your regular B or C exercise; rather, it should be added to your routine. Finally, whenever you perform substitute or supplemental exercises, be sure to do them in the same order as you do your regular exercises. In some cases an exercise may serve as a substitute for more than one muscle group.

GROUP I: LEGS

E. Supplement. CALF EXERCISE

Start: Stand with your toes on a fairly thick book (about two inches thick), heels on the floor, your arms at your sides.

Move: Raise your heels off the floor as high as possible, until you are standing on tiptoe on the book. Hold a moment, then slowly lower your heels to the floor. If you need support to keep your balance, *lightly* hold on to the wall or the back of a chair.

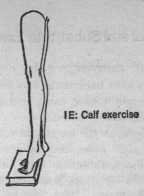

IE: Calf exercise

Goal: Start with two reps, build to sixteen. After you are used to the exercise, you can hold five-pound weights in each hand (overhand grip) to increase the resistance.

Comment: Don't use a phone book or paperback for this exercise—they aren't sturdy enough and may fall apart. Also, if you find the thickness of the book uncomfortable, use a thinner one at first. To minimize wear and tear on the book, stand on the side of the book that is bound. Finally, because many women have shortened calf muscles, it is especially important to do the calf stretcher (p. 62) as a warmup.

F. Substitute. JUMP ROPE

This is a good substitute for the bench step, because it also serves as an aerobic conditioning exercise. As with the bench step, begin with one minute of jumping and build up to ten; if you have been performing the bench step, begin with two minutes of jumping. Alternate feet as you jump to minimize jarring of your body and feet, and wear a pair of well-cushioned shoes. Jumping rope also helps to develop your arm, shoulder, and back muscles.

GROUP II: CHEST

F. Substitute. BENCH PRESS

Start: Lie on your back with your arms straight up in the air, a weight in each hand held in an overhand grip (your palms facing the ceiling).

Move: Slowly lower the weights to your upper chest, just above the collarbone, keeping your elbows close to your sides. Pause a moment, then push the weights straight up in the air again. Your arms should be perpendicular to the floor.

Suggested starting weight: Five to eight pounds. Start with two consecutive sets of six to eight reps each. Build to two sets of twelve reps, then go on to a heavier weight at two sets of six reps.

Goal: Two sets of twelve reps with a weight of ten or more pounds.

Comment: This exercise is traditionally performed

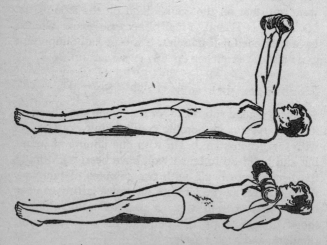

II F: Bench press (views 1 and 2)

on an exercise bench, using a barbell. If you have a very sturdy bench (such as a piano bench) that will support your body from the top of your head to your knees (which should be bent so that your feet can reach the floor), you can lie on it while doing this exercise. Alternatively, you could try stacking sofa cushions to make a lower, homemade bench. When performed flat on the floor, this exercise involves the triceps muscles to a much greater extent than when performed from a bench. When you lift from a bench or pillows, bring your bent elbows down as far as possible when you lower the weight to your upper chest.

GROUP III: UPPER BACK

E. Supplement. SHOULDER SHRUG

Start: Stand with your feet comfortably apart, arms at sides, holding a weight in each hand in an overhand grip (your palms facing your sides).

Move: Slowly raise your shoulders in a shrug (try to touch them to your ears), then lower them slowly, rolling the shoulders backwards. Do not bend your wrists or arms—try to think of them as dead weight to be moved by the shoulders.

Suggested starting weight: Five pounds. Start with two consecutive sets of six to eight reps each and build to two sets of twelve; then go on to a heavier weight at two sets of six reps.

Goal: Two sets of twelve reps with a weight of eight to ten or more pounds.

Comment: This exercise is considered to be the best single exercise for the trapezius muscles.

F. Substitute. BENT-OVER ROW

Start: Stand with your feet comfortably apart, your knees slightly bent. Bend forward from the waist until

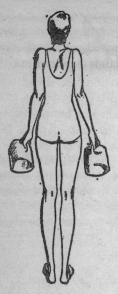

III E: Shoulder shrug

III F: Bent-over row

your trunk is parallel with the floor, your back straight, your arms hanging down with a weight in each hand in an overhand grip (your palms facing your legs).

Move: Slowly raise your hands, bringing the weights up until they touch your upper chest close to the shoulders. Your elbows should point up in the air.

Suggested starting weight: Three to five pounds. Start with two consecutive sets of six to eight reps each, build to two sets of twelve reps, then go on to a heavier weight at two sets of six reps.

Goal: Two sets of twelve reps each with a weight of eight to ten pounds.

Comment: This exercise is also good for your biceps (front of upper arm). However, if your biceps are still very weak, they will give out before your upper-back muscles have been thoroughly exercised. If this seems to be a problem for you, work on developing more arm strength before you substitute this exercise. This exercise can also be performed with a single weight held in both hands.

GROUP IV: LOWER BACK

F. *Substitute*. STIFF-LEGGED DEAD LIFT

Start: Stand with your feet comfortably apart, one weight held by both hands (use overhand or facing grip), your arms relaxed so that the weight is about at mid-thigh. Now bend over from the waist until the weight is resting on the floor, or is as close to the floor as you can manage.

Move: Come to a standing position, keeping your arms straight (you should try to think of your hands and arms—and the weights—as dead weight to be raised only by the action of your body). Keep your feet flat on the floor when you perform this exercise.

Suggested starting weight: Nine to ten pounds. Start with two consecutive sets of six to eight reps each, build to twelve reps, then move on to a heavier weight at six reps.

IV F: Stiff-legged dead lift

Goal: Two sets of twelve reps with a weight heavier than ten pounds (but not more than twenty).

Comment: If you have lower-back pain, check with your doctor before performing this lift. Also, if your starting weight causes pain, discontinue this exercise until your back is stronger.

GROUP V: SHOULDERS

F. Substitute. STANDING PRESS

Start: Stand with your feet comfortably apart, your back straight, and a weight in each hand at shoulder

VF: Standing press

level in an overhand grip (your palms facing forward).

Move: Slowly raise the right arm straight up until it is fully extended over your shoulder. Pause a moment, then slowly lower to starting position; *at the same time*, raise your left arm until it is fully extended. Continue, alternating arms.

Suggested starting weight: Two to three pounds. Start with two consecutive sets of six to eight reps each, build to two sets of twelve, then move on to a heavier weight at two sets of six to eight reps. (A rep counts each time your left arm returns to starting position.)

Goal: Two sets of twelve reps each with weights of five to eight pounds.

Comment: This exercise may also be performed holding the weight with your palms facing each other (still an overhand grip). For this reason, it is especially good if some of your weights consist of plastic jugs. Also, for variety, you may perform this exercise by lifting both arms together instead of alternating them, though this may be somewhat more difficult.

GROUP VI: FRONT OF UPPER ARMS

F. *Substitute*. NEGATIVE CHINUPS

This exercise is performed on the same principle as the negative pushup; i.e., a muscle is capable of lowering a great deal more weight than it can raise. It requires a chinning bar and is easier to perform if someone can assist you.

Start: Stand on a chair just under a chining bar, holding the bar in an underhand grip (your palms facing your body). Your hands should be shoulder-width apart, your chin just resting on the bar.

Move: Have the person assisting you move the chair

away, or kick it away yourself. Hang in the same position for three to five seconds; then slowly lower your body until you are hanging by your arms or until your feet touch the ground. Pick up the chair, put it back, return to starting position, and repeat.

Goal: Start with as many as you can do (for many women this will be as few as one), then build up to sixteen. Your ultimate goal is to do full chinups.

Comment: I realize that this exercise isn't a very practical one for most women, but if you have access to a chinning bar in a gym or a city playground, it is an excellent way to build strength in your biceps as well as in all forearm and gripping muscles. Most sporting goods stores sell adjustable doorway chinning bars for under ten dollars.

GROUP VII: BACKS OF UPPER ARMS

E. Supplement. STANDING PRESS (see p. 100) and BENCH PRESS (see p. 96)

F. Substitute. FRENCH CURL

Start: Lie on your back with your arms straight up in the air, one weight held between your hands (alternate, overhand grip, palms facing each other).

Move: Slowly—and carefully—lower the weight to the top of your head. Your elbows should be fairly close together and pointing straight up in the air. Pause, then raise the weight to starting position.

VII F: French curl

Suggested starting weight: Two to three pounds. Start with two consecutive sets of six to eight reps each, build to two sets of twelve reps, then go on to a heavier weight at six to eight reps for two sets.

Goal: Two sets of twelve reps, each with a weight of five to eight pounds.

Comment: As with the triceps press, while you perform this, try to keep your upper arms absolutely motionless. Only your forearms should move. Remember that one of the main functions of the triceps is to straighten your elbow, which it does in this exercise.

GROUP VIII: FOREARMS, WRISTS, HANDS

E. Supplement. BROOMSTICK WALK

Start: Stand comfortably, one arm straight out in front, holding the top of a broomstick (the broom is attached). The broom should be perpendicular to the floor.

Move: Using *only* your thumb and fingers, and keeping your arm outstretched, "walk" your hand down the broomstick to the bottom (that is, raise the broomstick until the broom part reaches your hand). Repeat with the other hand.

Goal: Start with as many as you can do and build to two complete reps with each hand. A rep counts as each time the broom part reaches your hand.

Comment: If you find this exercise too difficult, use a plain broomstick without the broom part attached, or only "walk" partway down, until your forearms are stronger.

F. Substitute. RUBBER BALL SQUEEZE

This exercise is simplicity itself. Get a fairly soft ball—an old tennis ball or even a tightly wound ball of yarn would serve. It should be soft enough for you to be able to squeeze it, yet hard enough to provide some resistance. Now squeeze the ball as tightly as you can for fifteen to thirty seconds. Relax, then repeat with the other hand. Do this two or three times with each hand.

GROUP IX: ABDOMEN

E. Supplement. SIDE BENDS

Start: Stand comfortably, arms at your sides, a weight held in each hand in an overhand grip (your palms facing your sides).

Move: Bend to one side as far as you can, letting your hand with the weight in it slide down your leg as far as possible. Hold a moment, return to start, then bend to the other side.

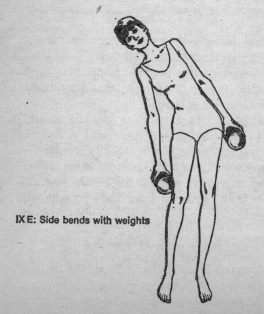

IX E: Side bends with weights

Suggested starting weight: See *Comment* below.

Goal: Start with twelve reps on each side; build to twenty-four on each side.

Comment: This exercise develops those abdominal muscles which are responsible for bending your body from side to side. You can perform the exercise with or without weights (weights will increase your strength more quickly), but bear in mind that if you use too heavy a weight (over five pounds), it can result in a slight thickening of your waistline as the muscle tissue builds up.

GROUP X: NECK (Optional)

The following exercises are strictly optional: that is, they needn't be added to the Basic Strength Program at all. However, for many sports (see Chapter Eleven, Getting Strong for Sports), neck strength is very important. Neck strength is also essential to good posture (see Chapter Ten). Further, the stronger your neck muscles, the better protected you are against neck injury. Bill Reynolds, author of *Complete Weight Training*, credits very strong neck muscles with having saved him from death or a broken neck during a serious motorcycle accident.

Part 1. FRONT OF NECK

Start: Sit on the floor, legs outstretched, your body bent slightly backward. Support yourself by stretching your arms out to the back and resting your hands on the floor behind you.

Move: Let your head drop back as far as possible, then slowly bring it up and forward until your chin is resting on your chest. Don't move your shoulders. Hold a moment, then return to start and repeat.

Goal: Start with twelve reps; build to twenty.

Part 2. BACK OF NECK

Start: Support yourself on your hands and knees, back straight.

Move: Let your head drop forward. Now slowly bring it up and back as far as you can. Don't move your shoulders. Hold a moment, then return to start. Repeat.

Goal: Start with twelve reps; build to twenty.

Part 3. SIDES OF NECK

Start: Sit comfortably on the floor or in a chair, back straight.

Move: Slowly lower your head to the right side as far as possible. Hold for a moment, then return to start. Now lower your head to the left side. Hold a moment, then return to start.

Goal: Start with twelve reps for each side; build to twenty on each side.

7

STICKING WITH IT

It may seem hard to believe, but some women actually enjoy exercise, even to the point of looking forward to it. Who are these demented, masochistic people? The surprising answer is that they are mostly women like me who have been exercising for a long period of time. Although some lucky women enjoy workouts from the very first session, they are more the exception than the rule.

In my own case, I never did any physical exercise in my entire life until I was twenty-nine; it was then that I began jogging, and three years later I added the weight-training sessions. Though I enjoy both these activities now and consider them the high points of my day, that wasn't always so. When I first started, I shared the fears and misgivings that all new exercisers feel: dread of pain, of exertion, and of boredom.

Boredom is one of the most common reasons—or excuses—given by those who are reluctant to begin an exercise program. The sad fact is that your exercise sessions often *will* be boring, at least for the first few workouts. Because you are making new demands on muscles that are not accustomed to strenuous activity, you are particularly aware of the effort and repetition involved, and these sensations may be interpreted by your brain as boredom.

Still, a lot of that boredom may come from your attitude toward the exercise: if you expect it to be dreary, it probably will be. While the converse isn't always the case—that is, telling yourself that exercise will be a wonderful, stimulating experience doesn't guarantee that you'll find it so—you can still influence your attitude in a positive way. As my friend Carol put it, "When I decided to start doing the program, I made up my mind to approach the exercises from the beginning as something pleasurable, something that feels good. And they were." It is also important to keep the *purpose* of the exercises in mind. You are working out to improve your strength, endurance, flexibility, and appearance, *not* to fill fifteen minutes with mentally stimulating activity.

However, as anyone who has worked out regularly for any period of time can tell you, the longer you continue to exercise, the less aware you will be of any boredom. With weight training—as with jogging, swimming, or even hitting tennis balls against a wall —the sense of tedium lessens after a while. The reasons that this happens are complex and not completely understood, but I think part of the answer is that as physical activity becomes a regular part of your life, your whole body begins to look forward to it. As you get better at the exercises, not only do you feel a sense of accomplishment as you see your strength improve, but the actual working of the muscles during the exercises starts to feel natural and good. I now find that each successive workout feels better than the last, and that the joy of effort involved in my weight training is almost as important to me as the overall results in terms of strength and appearance. My attitude toward the exercise itself is now positive—and that makes it hard to be bored.

How long does it take for the exercise to begin to feel good? Of course it will vary from woman to woman; to a large extent it will depend on how fit you are when you begin the program and how regularly you work out. If you exercise only occasionally, each new workout is almost like beginning anew. The key to rapid progress both physically and mentally is to do your workouts *regularly:* three times a week, every week, even if you have to force yourself at first. After four to six weeks, your body will be accustomed to the routine of exercise and you will begin to feel the joy of effort and a corresponding diminishing of boredom.

When you first begin, you may have to take these assurances on faith. Until exercise has become a firmly ingrained habit, you'll probably have to exert a little extra will power to get yourself to do the workouts. But bear in mind that a large component of will power is attitude. If you find yourself approaching a workout with dread, try to examine that feeling. What are you dreading? Boredom? Boredom is nothing to be afraid of and will soon go away. Pain? The pain of a workout is slight and transitory—in fact, some people find this kind of pain pleasurable. Are you afraid of the effort involved? Well, you will have to exert effort, but effort is nothing to fear, just something to be aware of. In short, you have nothing to fear but fear itself, at least where your physical fitness is concerned.

Even after exercise has become a firmly established habit, there will still be days when you just won't feel like exercising or when the exercise session itself will be unpleasant. All women who work out regularly have these occasional down days, and most of us have devised ways of coping with them. To help you get past those times, as well as to help you over the first few weeks of the program, here are some suggestions that I and other women in the training program have found useful. Read through these suggestions and try the ones you think will work for you. And bear in mind that the amount of time you spend getting strong, and later staying strong, is a very small amount of time out of your entire life—as little as 45 out of the 10,080 minutes in your week. That's not much discomfort for such worthwhile results.

Make Yourself Comfortable

This might seem too elementary even to mention, but a lot of people still approach all physical exercise with a spartan-like attitude. With their preconceived idea that exercise has to be a rigid, unpleasant routine, something to force themselves through, these women don't do anything to make it agreeable.

How can you make yourself comfortable? First of all, be sure to wear something comfortable, something loose and soft. And keep in mind that appearance can be part of comfort, too. If you're feeling particularly down, exercising in a brightly colored T-shirt or your new bathing suit can give your spirits a lift. Secondly, make your environment as pleasant as possible. Working out generates a lot of body heat. When you do your exercise routine, make sure that your environment is cool (the most comfortable temperature is 65°F). If it's winter, open a window slightly. Even if you shiver at first, very soon you will be sweating—and grateful for that breath of fresh air.

In the summer it's even more important to keep cool. I have a friend who began the Basic Strength Program in the middle of New York's worst heat wave in twenty-five years. It's obviously not a good idea to start an exercise regimen during such unusual weather conditions, and Nancy didn't do anything to make it easier for herself. "I'm sorry," she told me after only three weeks on the program. "I had to give it up. It's just too hot to exercise." I asked her whether she had a fan, and she said yes, but the fan was in her bedroom, and she did her workout in the living room. Well, then, I asked, why didn't she move the fan into the living room for her workout?

"Oh, it's too much trouble," she said.

I think it would probably have added about two minutes to her exercise routine to unplug the fan from the bedroom and move it into the living room while she worked out. But she was not interested in making herself comfortable while she exercised; instead, she wanted to jump right in and get it over with. With an attitude like that, it's no wonder she was ready to give up the whole idea of exercise.

Although Nancy still hasn't returned to her strength-building program, I haven't given up on her. It took me three years of setting a good example to get her to start running, and as I continue to increase my muscular strength and endurance, I make sure she knows about it. I've also given her a standing invitation to work out in front of *my* fan any time she wants.

The moral of this story is clear: make comfort a top priority. Whether it involves changing the temperature of the room or simply dimming the lights, you'll find the workout far more pleasant, and you'll be more likely to look forward to it.

Distract Yourself

Okay, now you're comfortable. But you're still bored —or afraid you will be. Well, since boredom is, according to the dictionary, a state of mental fatigue induced by repetition or tediousness, try keeping your mind occupied.

Many of the women I know who work out do so to

music. Not only can music distract your mind, its rhythms can make your exercises easier to perform. My friend Phyllis reports that she tends to get carried away sometimes, particularly on her leg exercises: "I put on some music and go with it, and the next thing I know it's practically like dancing. Sometimes I overdo and I'm really sore the next day, but it's fun. I never get bored."

Another woman always plays classical music while she works out, "though sometimes it backfires. The station I listen to has some weird deejays, and every once in a while they put on something like Gregorian chants, which totally blows my concentration."

If the surprising tastes of a deejay create problems for you, then put on your favorite record. One woman I know welcomes the exercise session as a chance to reminisce with her record collection. "I have these hundreds of old records that I haven't listened to in years," she explains. "Now, every time I work out, I pull out a different old record. It's really fun—it takes me back to my childhood and makes the exercises go really fast. I'm into my folky period now—just started on my old Kingston Trio collection. Since my workout lasts just about exactly the length of one side of a record album, it's going to be months before I get through all of them."

Another good way to distract yourself is to listen to an all-news radio station, if your town has one. Or schedule your workout in the evening, during the nightly TV news. I do this at least once a week, and I find that the distraction works both ways: not only does watching Walter Cronkite make my workout go by quickly, but the fact that I'm exerting myself physically makes the impact of the daily news much less depressing.

Although distracting yourself will make exercising easier, don't carry it too far: remember that you should

always be concentrating enough on the exercises themselves so that you will perform them properly.

Don't Get into a Rut

Anyone can become bored with the same old routine, day in and day out. For this reason I think it's
important to vary your exercise regimen. For instance,
if you always do the B exercise for a specific muscle
group, switch to the C or a supplemental exercise, at
least once in a while. Or even drop one exercise
occasionally.

It's also a good idea occasionally to change the
number of reps you do. If you are getting tired of a
certain exercise, try performing it for a lower number
of reps with heavier weight, or for a higher number
of reps with lighter weight.

After you have completed the minimum goals for
the program or reached your own goals, it's even more
important to switch exercises from time to time. For
one thing, switching exercises will develop the same
muscle groups in slightly different ways, and for another it will keep any one exercise from becoming
stale.

Although I stated earlier that it's a good idea to
schedule your workout for about the same time every
day, you needn't be a slave to this routine. If it works
out better for you to exercise sometimes in the morning and sometimes in the evening, then by all means
make that your schedule. And once you have achieved
your goals and are performing maintenance, it's even
all right to take a vacation from exercise for a week
or two, as long as you start on a lower level in the
program when you get back to it.

The important thing is to be flexible. If you always
exercise on Monday, Wednesday, and Friday, try

switching to Tuesday, Thursday, and Sunday. If you always exercise in the living room, try working out in the bedroom or even the kitchen, if there is room.

Another good idea, at least for those who live in temperate climates, is to exercise outdoors sometimes. If you have access to a lawn, you won't even need your exercise mat—just a large towel. And if you work out in your bikini, you can get started on a suntan at the same time.

Tailor the Program to *You*

Since you know yourself better than anyone else, only you can discover the best ways to stick with your exercise program from day to day and week to week. Don't be afraid to experiment. For example, if you're having a great deal of trouble completing your routine on a given day, try resting longer between sets. Do the exercises more slowly. Or cut down on your usual number of reps. And don't feel bad about it—chances are you'll be back to normal by your next exercise session.

If you're the sort of person who tends to put things off, don't leave yourself time to procrastinate. My friend Lois advises, "I used to do my workout in the evening, but I kept putting it off so long that all of a sudden it was bedtime. So I moved my workout to the first thing in the morning, and that seems to work much better. There's no way I can procrastinate now, because I'll be late for work if I do. I just get up, brush my teeth, wash my face, and get strong."

The idea of moving your workout to the morning may work especially well if you tend to be a "day person," because you will probably be more energetic in the morning and thus have a better workout. I'm just the opposite—a true night person who feels seriously tormented if forced to get up before nine in the morning. Making a cup of coffee without burning down the kitchen is usually the most demanding morning activity I can manage. Naturally, I schedule my workout in the evening.

A final suggestion, particularly as you approach or have achieved the goals for the program: once you have proved to yourself that you can get strong and once you know how good the exercises make you feel, you will probably find it easier to continue if you buy dumbbells or adjustable dumbbells. This is especially important if you think the awkwardness of homemade weights is preventing you from achieving all that you want to on the program.

Get Strong With Friends

Although you may not be able to schedule every single workout with someone else, it can be fun to exercise with friends, at least sometimes. Furthermore, if you know that someone is counting on you at five o'clock every Thursday afternoon to work out with her, it makes it a lot harder to find excuses.

Exercising with friends can also be a practical idea. For one thing, you can share weights. I used to work out occasionally with a friend who has dumbbells: we used my homemade weights for exercises requiring lighter weights, and her ten-pound dumbbells when we needed something heavier. It was also fun (though sometimes discouraging) to compare our progress on the different exercises.

On the other hand, some women are inhibited by having other people around while they are working out. Since in some circles the idea of a woman's wanting to improve her strength is still considered only slightly less bizarre than trying to teach chimpanzees to talk (an effort, incidentally, which is under way in scientific laboratories all over the country), you may find yourself more self-conscious than usual, particularly if the observer is a man. My friend Phyllis reports that she has a hard time completing her routine when her husband is around. "He doesn't say or do anything to undermine me," she says. "But I find I often start undermining *myself*—I'll start to laugh or something because I feel so silly. Did you ever try to lift weights while you're laughing?"

I had a similar problem myself early in my program, when my boyfriend came over one afternoon while I was working out. I had told him what I was planning to do—to get strong by lifting cans of tomato juice and bottles of water. Knowing me, he had long since resigned himself to the fact that I was likely to do almost anything. But I could tell that he wasn't quite ready to watch me do biceps curls with two large cans of V-8 when he made a strangled sound and rushed into the other room so I wouldn't hear his laughter. The following week I got my revenge: I finally beat him at paddle ball.

Keep a Record

I cannot overemphasize the importance of keeping a record of your workouts: when you exercised, how much weight you lifted, how many sets and reps you did, how you felt. Not only will the record help you keep track of your progress, it can help keep you going through those periods when you are feeling blah about the whole idea of exercise. If you wake up one day thinking, "Who needs this?" you can often reawaken your interest by going back over your exercise record. Seeing yourself change from a weakling who could only lift two pounds to a Wonder Woman who is easily pumping fifteen or more pounds at a time not only does a lot for your self-esteem, but can provide just the boost you need to get back to that exercise mat.

You can keep records on an exercise log like the sample in this book, or you can make your own. Some women keep a loose-leaf notebook with detailed notes on their workouts: how they felt, body measurements, etc. Whatever sort of log you decide on, I urge you to go out as soon as possible and photocopy several blank exercise sheets. Otherwise you may run into the problem reported by one woman who had finished the minimal goals of the Basic Strength Program. "I loved it—I mean I even found the exercises fun, and it was a gas to actually get stronger. But then I used up all the spaces on my exercise sheet, and I kept putting off getting a new one, and the first thing I knew, I was out of the habit of exercising."

Trick Yourself

If all else fails, trick yourself. My friend Louise admits she does this sometimes. "If I really don't feel like exercising," she says, "I tell myself I'll just start . . . and if I still don't feel like it after one set I can quit for the day. Somehow, I've never yet quit after getting started. Once I get out the equipment and put on my leotard, it seems silly not to finish the workout, especially since it takes such a short time. And afterward I'm always glad I did."

Another woman uses a variation on this approach: she does her workouts in the evenings after work. On the day her workout is scheduled, she assembles all the equipment in the morning and puts it in her living room on top of her exercise mat. "Since that's the first thing I see when I come home, it's easy to get myself to work out," she says. "All I do is take off my clothes, go into the living room, and do my exercises. The only time it backfired was one evening when I invited a friend over for a drink after work. I forgot I had the stuff laid out. He gave me a very strange look when he saw cans of food and bottles of water all over the floor."

Psych Yourself Up

I keep emphasizing the importance of attitude in starting and sticking with an exercise program because I am convinced that your attitude will determine your ultimate success or failure in this or any other regimen. And you can influence your own attitude to a remarkable extent just by talking to yourself, literally or mentally. After I had developed my Basic Strength Program I enlisted the aid of a number of women friends and acquaintances to help me test it. Not all stuck with it, of course, but of those who did I was struck by the number of women who told me: "I really enjoyed the sense of doing something for myself."

My friend Carol is a case in point. "I do the exercises slowly and really put all of my mind into every sensation that I am feeling. I tell myself I'm getting in touch with my body—and it works."

A co-worker told me that she always used to go home after work and have a beer to pamper herself. Now she goes home and works out instead, and she says she feels for the first time in her life as if she really *is* pampered, because for the first time she is doing something that makes her body feel good.

Remind yourself of all the positive results of the effort you're putting in. One woman I know tells me, "At first I found it hard to stick with the program. I couldn't see any results. But then one day I suddenly realized that the waistbands on all of my slacks and skirts were too loose. I measured myself—and sure enough, I'd lost about an inch off my waist. Then my husband told me that I seemed to have put more *on* my bust. I guess there was really nothing there but muscle, but the program brought it out. So now when I'm not in the mood to exercise, I just tell myself that if I don't, I'll go back to being flat-chested and thick-waisted—and I have no problem getting out the weights."

Another way of psyching yourself up is to tell yourself how good you'll feel after you do the exercise. Sometimes when I'm feeling particularly lazy, I use this method. I know from experience that the reason I'm feeling lazy usually is just that my body needs a workout. So I tell myself how relaxed and energetic I'll feel after I do the exercises, and it always proves to be true. And when it's over I often go out and run for fifteen or twenty minutes.

The flip side of this approach, of course, is to tell yourself how bad you'll feel if you *don't* exercise. While I generally think it's a bad idea to make yourself feel guilty for any reason, sometimes it provides just the extra bit of motivation you need to get going.

Be Proud of Yourself

Remember how good you felt in grade school when your mother praised the ceramic ashtray you had carefully crafted out of clay? You were proud of yourself, and you had good reason to be: you had created something beautiful out of something ordinary. Similarly, by getting strong, you are creating a more beautiful, more capable, and healthier body—and you have as much right to be proud of yourself now as you did back in fourth grade. So allow yourself to feel that pride—and to show it. Brag or even show off a little: by getting strong you've earned the right to display what a co-worker of mine refers to as "muscle macha."

Louise, who lifts a fifty-pound bicycle up and down a flight of stairs every day, says that with very little provocation she enjoys " 'making a muscle' for anyone who hints at my frailty. All kinds of small and large daily activities are easier. Grocery shopping is a snap. Canoeing goes effortlessly. Carrying a heavy suitcase through Penn Station is now a simple task. All this muscle building leads to female chauvinism!"

Lynne, a young editor, is another convert to muscle macha. This is manifested in her secretly "getting a kick out of leaving my dumbbells lying around my apartment for anyone to see.

"I'm enjoying a new feeling of power," she says. "My dreams of frustration used to involve my trying to punch someone—but never being able to connect. Soon after starting the program, I dreamed for the first time that I connected! (And the dreams stopped plaguing me.)"

Whether or not you develop a raging case of muscle macha, I think you will find, as so many other women are discovering, not only that the good effects of getting strong reinforce the reasons for exercising, but that they lead to other, sometimes surprising physical developments. As Ellen puts it, "Whole new horizons open up. My getting strong led to my trying backpacking, which led to cross-country skiing, and now I'm thinking of taking a wilderness survival course— where a whole lot more than strength and endurance is involved. I used to be a timid person, physically and mentally. Now I'm just the opposite—sometimes I think I could probably do anything."

Lynne also says she's noticing new reasons for getting strong. Carpentry had always seemed beyond her because it was performed with heavy power tools.

Now she feels that she is capable of developing not only the strength but the skills to handle the tools. Another woman I know is about to enroll in a fencing class—something she has wanted to do for years— and is confident that her new strength and endurance will help her to be good at the sport.

Staying Strong for Life

My friend Terry once asked me why, when I have so many other things to do, I wanted to get strong. After I'd explained all the reasons to her, she said, "I guess I can see why you want to do it. But I never could. I just don't have time."

Terry, however, *does* have time to manicure her nails once a week, and to blow-dry her long hair each morning. It's partly a question of priorities: I too try to make time for my nails when I can, but exercising is so much more important in my life that if anything has to go, it's not going to be my workouts—running and getting strong. The reason is that exercise has become a natural, deeply ingrained part of my life— as much a habit as brushing my teeth in the morning. It wasn't easy to make it so important—if by "easy" we mean "without effort." But it wasn't all that hard, either. All it really took was a determination to stick to it for a few weeks, until the routine itself had become a firmly imbedded habit, as difficult to break as any other habit. And that ultimately is the key to staying strong for life—to make your workouts so natural and important to your mind and your body that you would no more think of giving them up than you would consider giving up breathing.

8

QUESTIONS WOMEN ASK
ABOUT WEIGHT TRAINING

In a very real sense, modern female athletes are pioneers—not only because there have been so few of us until recently, but because historically the (mostly male) experts concentrated mainly on male athletes and their problems and needs. Less is known about the needs and problems of women, and because of our own limited experience with physical activity, we tend to know less about ourselves and our physical responses.

Following are answers to questions that are frequently asked about this program, about weight training in general, and about special problems that apply to women only.

How can I be sure I'm doing the exercises correctly?

It is extremely important to perform all weight-training exercises with the correct technique; many or all of the benefits may be lost otherwise. For any given exercise, study the drawings and read the instructions carefully. It might also be helpful to work out with someone else the first few times, so you can observe each other. And again, working out in front of a full-length mirror will allow you to see what you are doing for most exercises. For the first few weeks on the program, it might also be helpful to read the section on weight training (Chapter Four, pp. 41–59) from time to time, and to review the section on muscles (Chapter Three, pp. 23–40), so you can learn to visualize what each muscle group is supposed to do in each exercise.

Finally, if you are still uncertain or are having special trouble with one or more exercises, you might take a copy of this book with you to a gym or Y and ask someone there to observe you while you work out.

How do I know when it's time to use a heavier weight?

As I mentioned earlier, when you can do more than twelve reps with a given weight, that weight has become too light for you. In general, the first few reps of an exercise should be fairly easy, but succeeding reps should become progressively harder, because of fatigue. Thus, the last rep should be performed *with correct technique* only with great difficulty, and when you have finished it, ideally your muscles will be too tired to perform even one more complete rep without a rest. When you build to twelve reps for a set and that last rep becomes easier and your muscles aren't too tired to go on to a thirteenth, it's time to move on to a heavier weight and a lower number of reps.

There may be days when you find yourself feeling especially strong. On a day like this you might try the next heavier weight at a lower number of reps. Sometimes the ease or difficulty of lifting a heavier weight is more psychological than physiological.

I want to use a heavier weight, but I find that the next-heavier weight I have is too heavy to do even one more rep with.

This is a common problem for many women on a weight-training program. Most dumbbell sets come in weights of three, five, and ten pounds. Even adjustable dumbbells are usually adjustable only in leaps of two and a half or more pounds. While a man in good condition probably won't have any problem with the jump from, say, five to ten pounds, this can be a real burden for women who are very weak.

I solved this problem for myself on Exercise IIIB, one of the hardest of the exercises for me, with home-made weights. I had progressed from one-pound cans to two- and three-pound cans, and finally five-pound bottles, but my next heaviest weight was eight pounds, and no matter how many sets and reps I did with five pounds, I could not make the leap to eight. Then one day in the supermarket I saw a three-quart bottle that weighed six pounds. This turned out to be just the increment I needed, and after a few weeks with this weight I was able to go on to eight. (And with six quarts of fabric softener on hand, I'm assured of years of soft, fluffy clothing.)

Another solution to this problem, on those exercises where only one weight is used (or those where one weight *can* be used, such as the lying overhead lift), is to use what is called a swingbell—a miniature barbell. If you have a set of adjustable dumbbells, you can make a swingbell by putting one or more weight plates in the center of the bar and securing them on either side. Then hold the weight by grasping the ends of the bars.

Try experimenting with different weights and combinations of weights. Also, if you buy your equipment, shop around. You may be able to find adjustable dumbbells with very lightweight plates. Overall, I think this problem is best solved with a combination of store-bought and homemade equipment, at least in the early stages of the program.

Speaking of homemade weights . . . I find them awkward to hold.

Another common complaint. So do I, at least sometimes, and I tend more and more to use dumbbells for my workouts. But changing the plates on adjustable dumbbells can be time-consuming. Again, I think the most practical approach is to use a combination of the two types of weights, at least until you become so strong that you don't need any light weights at all. Almost anyone can hold cans or bottles of one to three pounds without much difficulty.

My left side is so much weaker than my right side that I don't know what weight to use. I can easily lift five pounds with my right hand, but I have to struggle to lift even two with my left hand.

Most of us are stronger on one side than the other—on the right side for right-handers. When you first begin the program, you needn't worry about this discrepancy too much: choose a weight that you can handle for the weaker side (but one that will really challenge it). The weaker side will become stronger much more quickly than the stronger side, and soon the difference should be minimal or will disappear altogether.

If, after several weeks on the program, you still find a marked discrepancy in the strength of the two sides of your body, try adding an *extra set* for the weaker side after your regular workout for each muscle group where imbalance is a problem. This is in the nature of a remedial exercise and should quickly help to bring the weaker side to normal.

Why do situps hurt my back?

Situps shouldn't hurt your back if you are doing them correctly: that is, slowly, keeping your *lower back flat on the floor*, and consciously curling your body up and then curling it down. Remember that the curling principle applies whether you are raising your whole body or just the head and neck. The movement should be slow and smooth—no jerking as you come up. Be sure to keep your chin tucked and your back *rounded*. In my case, I used to get back pains on the last few reps of situps. An expert advised me to slow down, and it worked. I realized I'd been rushing through this exercise because I didn't like it, and thus I was not doing it correctly the last few reps. Now that I concentrate on slow performance with correct form, I like the exercise a lot better, and it doesn't hurt.

If you try the above suggestions and still have lower-back pain, try cutting down on your reps until your abdominal muscles are stronger. If you are now doing your situps with your hands behind your head, it may also help to cross them over your chest instead. Finally, if you absolutely can't sit up without feeling a pain in your back, then perform only the half-situp (IXA, p. 83).

When I do situps, my tailbone gets sore. How can I prevent that?

I have this problem too—it comes from being thin and bony, and the best solution I have found is to place extra cushioning under my back and buttocks when I do situps; I use a folded towel in addition to my exercise mat for this exercise. If tailbone pain becomes a serious problem for you, cut down on your reps or substitute the following exercise for situps:

BENT-LEGGED LEG LIFTS

Start: Lie on your back, your knees bent, your hands folded underneath your head.

Move: Bring your knees to your shoulders, trying to get your hips off the floor. At the same time raise your head and tuck your chin into your chest. Hold for three to five seconds, then return to start. Repeat.

Goal: Start with as many as you can do; build to twenty-five reps.

Comment: If you are doing this correctly, you will feel a burning sensation in the lower part of your abdomen. This exercise primarily strengthens the *lower* part of the abdominal muscles, while situps strengthen the *upper* part.

Why do my muscles sometimes tremble while I am working out?

Muscular trembling while you are working out is merely a sign of fatigue—and an indication that your muscles are working hard. It is nothing to worry about and should become less of a problem as you become stronger and build more endurance. Even very strong athletes sometimes tremble when seriously challenging their muscles—as can easily be seen in weight-lifting competitions.

What happens if I stop doing the Basic Strength Program?

The main thing is that you will lose some of the muscular conditioning you have built up so far. This will not happen immediately or all at once; in fact, the stronger you have become on the program, the longer you will maintain a measure of your strength. Still, sooner or later, you will return to your former level of unfitness.

Will my muscles turn to fat?

This is a common belief, probably based on the correct observation that some conditioned athletes, such as football players and weight lifters, tend to become fat and flabby as they quit their sports and grow older. This happens, of course, precisely *because* they have given up their sports; anyone who continues to work out will continue to be fit.

Muscle cannot turn to fat any more than lead can turn to gold; muscle is one kind of tissue and fat is another kind. What actually happens is that when muscles are not worked out, their conditioning is lost and they become smaller: the area that the muscle mass occupied may now be taken up by fat, especially if you eat as much as you did when you were working out, since the excess calories will now be stored as fat instead of being burned.

Is weight training a good way to build coordination for sports?

Yes, indeed. Although coordination for any particular sport is *best* improved through practicing the movements in that sport, the strength and endurance you gain from a weight-training program will help to improve your overall coordination.

Endurance is particularly important for any activity in which coordination is important. I noticed after I had been on the Basic Strength Program for a while that I was applying nail polish more easily and with less smearing. I asked a physiologist whether there might be a connection between strength and the precision control of my hand. He replied that while some of it might be psychological (relating to improved self-esteem), the key was probably that the endurance of my hands, wrists, upper arms, and shoulders had improved, so that I fatigued far less readily and therefore had more control for a longer period of time. Thus, since my hands are getting tired less readily, I'm able to apply my second and third coats of polish with as much control as the first. A photographer friend began working on getting strong so that she would be able to hold her camera steady for longer periods of time; she reports that it seems to be working.

This effect of endurance is particularly noticeable in sports in which you need to manipulate equipment. Getting strong improved my paddle-ball backhand both in the strength of my shots and in my ability to wield the paddle with control for an entire game. A friend who lifts weights told me that he often beats tennis or golf partners in the later stages of a game: though they may be more skilled at the sport than he is, he is able to maintain his control longer and is often more accurate on the final holes or sets.

Should I work out if I'm sick?

There are some athletes who make a fetish out of engaging in their sport or exercise under all kinds of adverse conditions, including illness. On the other hand, there are those who will use almost any excuse to avoid a workout. The best answer to this question is to use common sense. If you aren't too sick—if you have a mild cold, for example—there is probably no harm in working out, and the physical activity will very likely make you feel a little better.

But if you're really sick—that is, if you're running a fever or you feel so awful that you can barely drag yourself around—why add more stress to your body? Instead, go to bed, drink orange juice, and don't even think about exercising until you feel better. Even if you lose a little ground on the program, you'll soon be able to catch up.

Can I exercise during my period?

For too many years, there has been a prevalent myth that women should exert themselves as little as possible during their periods, as if menstruation were somehow an abnormal condition. Current research indicates that all phases of menstrual difficulties—from premenstrual tension to menstrual cramps—are eased or even eliminated with regular exercise. I have spoken to dozens of women for whom this has proved to be true.

As for exercising while you're actually experiencing cramps—it's up to you, but try it as an experiment. I've found that the more physical activity I can make myself perform during those times, the better I usually feel.

What about pregnancy?

If you are now pregnant, this is not the time to *begin* any sort of exercise program. But most doctors today agree that if you have been exercising regularly, you can continue to maintain the level of exercise that is *normal for you* throughout your pregnancy. When you ask your obstetrician's advice, be sure to tell her exactly what your exercise program involves, so she will best be able to advise you.

Can older women do the Basic Strength Program?

Women of any age can begin conditioning programs, but the older you are, the more important it is to check with your doctor before starting unaccustomed physical activity. This is important not only because of the decreasing elasticity of our tissues as we get older, but also because women past menopause are particularly subject to a condition known as osteoporosis, or brittle bones. (Research indicates, by the way, that an important cause of this condition is inactivity; therefore, the more active you are as a young woman, the less likely you are to develop this potentially crippling disease as you get older.)

My aunt has osteoporosis, which has resulted in several broken bones in recent years. While trying to get into shape after having convalesced from a broken pelvis, she was too enthusiastic in performing calisthenics one morning and broke two ribs. The point is that the older you are, the more cautious you should be. Also, older women should start with lighter weights than those suggested for the Basic Program; this is because you have had a longer time for your muscles to become weak.

9

GETTING THIN: DIET
AND FIGURE CONTROL

Fashions in figures change from age to age and from
society to society. Where food is scarce, a premium is
often put on excess body weight, as a sign of prosper-
ity. If you're rolling in blubber, the theory goes, you
must be doing very well indeed.

In other societies, such as our own, where an over-
abundance of food is available to those who can afford
it, the opposite is the case: to be fashionable in America today, you must be skinny. The higher up the
social ladder you go, in fact, the higher the proportion
of gaunt men and women. But, fashion aside, there is
a great deal of evidence that thinner people live
longer. In studies done on rats, it was found that a
semi-starvation diet somehow slowed the aging process and produced a group of very long-lived rats (who
also matured much later than their normally fed
counterparts). And everyone has read of centenarians
in the Soviet Union and the mountains of Central
America who live on very meager diets of grains,
legumes, and a small amount of animal protein. One
would assume, therefore, that the upper echelons of
American society must be one of the healthiest and
longest-lived groups in history.

While this may be true for some affluent men and women, it is obviously not true for the majority of Americans, male or female: high blood pressure and heart disease are practically national epidemics. Those primitive Indian and mountain peoples with the long lives are thin and healthy, yes; but they also eat a diet low in saturated animal fats, they lead lives fairly free from the kinds of stress that most Americans must face, and most important of all, they are physically active from the cradle to the grave. Although getting thin may be a laudable goal, it's not going to do you much good if you achieve that goal by crash dieting, popping pills, or upping your cigarette consumption, all while you sit around watching television.

About one third of all American women and nearly one half of all American men are overweight. But even these high figures don't tell the full story. If you are carrying fifteen or more pounds too many, you probably know it, because those pounds show and they affect the way you feel. But what about those people who may not know that they are actually too fat? I'm sure you're familiar with one of those fortunate and envy-provoking people who brag that they can eat three plates of spaghetti every single evening and never gain an ounce. Yet even these people may actually be too fat. This is because dress sizes and the height-weight charts tell only one story: they do not tell you what proportion of your body is made up of fat.

The percentage of body fat is a secondary sexual characteristic, as is the distribution of that fat: in women, extra fat is usually carried on the hips, buttocks, and abdomen (surprise!), and it is normal and desirable up to a point. How much fat should you have? Well, the answer varies from person to person, but in general, the "normal" percentage of body fat is fifteen percent of body weight for men and twenty percent for women. Anything beyond this is too much and constitutes obesity. Most trained athletes have lower percentages of body fat than the norm, although the lower limit for well-trained women is about ten percent.

It is possible to be overweight without being "overfat"—for example, a very large football player may seem to weigh too much for his height, yet that weight is in heavy bones and firm, conditioned muscle. But the condition of being "overfat"—with or without excess weight—is far more common and unhealthy. Unless you are physically active, you may have too much fat even if your weight is within the normal range.

How can you tell whether you have more than the desirable amount of fat on your body? If your weight is within the "normal" range for your height— that is, if you can't actually see the extra fat—the easiest way to tell is to do the pinch test. Take a fold of flesh between your thumb and forefinger, then slide your thumb and forefinger off the pinch of skin and measure (or estimate) the distance between them. To make sure you are pinching only skin and fat, pinch fairly firmly. Muscle is more solid than fat, which feels squishy and light. If the distance between your thumb and forefinger is more than three quarters of an inch, you are carrying too much fat on your body. The best places to check for excess fat are the backs of your upper arms, the front of your abdomen at navel level, and the fronts of your thighs.

If you want to reduce the amount of weight, the percentage of body fat, or both, the most sensible and the easiest way to do it, as well as the way that is most likely to have long-term results, is to combine a gradual and well-balanced diet with exercise.

So far, so good. Those of you who want to lose only a little bit of weight or who merely want to firm unconditioned flab are probably nodding and saying, "Fine. Let's get started." But what about those women with a lifelong weight problem centering around compulsive eating? If you have a compulsion to eat, I don't have to tell you that it's not easy to lose weight. However, it can be done, as countless foodoholics can testify. And it can be done most readily and easily with the help of exercise, as the experience of my former roommate Kathleen shows.

For the first twenty-nine years of her life, Kathleen fought a losing battle with food. In the fifteen years I've known her, I've watched her gain and lose literally hundreds of pounds through all kinds of regimens, from miracle crash diets to sensible group plans. Nothing ever worked, even though she knew intellectually that the answer was to change her eating and living habits. Then she combined going to a diet counselor with vigorous exercise (in her case, calisthenics and running) and for the past year I have watched her almost day by day become more beautiful. Not only is she now fashionably thin, but she has also become more healthy, emotionally as well as physically, by proving to herself that she can really do it. The diet counselor is both helping her to understand why she has a need to overeat and providing positive reinforcement while she retrains her eating habits. The exercise is helping her to burn excess calories and is reshaping her body, as flabby fat is replaced with firm muscle. Kathleen feels sure (and so do I) that this time she has found the answer to lifelong weight control.

What about you? Whether your goal is to lose fifty pounds or more or simply to rid your body of some percentage of excess fat, exercise combined with diet may be your answer.

Myths About Exercise and Weight Loss

There are a lot of mistaken notions about exercise and diet. The most prevalent and perhaps the most false is that if you step up your level of exercise, your appetite will automatically increase and you may end up actually *gaining* weight.

Like all myths, this one has a germ of truth in it: occasional mild exercise can indeed have the effect of temporarily stimulating your appetite. For example, suppose you are a normally sedentary woman who one day goes on a picnic in the woods and spends a few minutes hiking around. Since you're not used to any exercise at all, the unaccustomed exertion may cause you to come back to the campfire starved, and you'll probably stuff yourself—and who could blame you? Any moderate exercise, such as spending a day in the garden—if you aren't used to it—can make you somewhat hungrier than usual. If you give in to the temptation to satisfy that hunger, you may well take in more food than is good for you.

But remember—we are talking here about *occasional* moderate exercise. More vigorous exercise, especially that which is performed regularly, has the opposite effect: it tends to decrease the appetite. We will examine some of the reasons for this later, but this effect of exercise is well known to runners, swimmers, cyclists—indeed anyone on a regular, vigorous exercise program. After a hard workout, the last thing anyone wants is a big, rich meal.

So, exercise won't increase your appetite. But how much good can it do? After all, you have to do a lot of it to make a difference, right? This is another common myth about exercise and weight loss, and again, there is a grain of truth in it. It's obvious that exercise burns calories, but you may have heard that you must perform a great deal of exercise to burn a significant number of calories. For example, running or walking one mile uses approximately a hundred calories. (I know this sounds incredible, but no matter how fast or slowly you do that mile, it's still about a hundred calories' worth of exercise.) Since one pound of fat represents thirty-five hundred stored calories, you would therefore have to run or walk thirty-five miles to lose a pound! With statistics like that, it's no wonder more dieters don't exercise to lose weight.

Like many statistics, though, this one is misleading. Of course no one but a marathoner in training is even going to consider going out and running (or walking) thirty-five miles all at once. But suppose you break that thirty-five miles down into small segments—say, by walking a mile and a half a day. In less than twenty-four days you will have used up thirty-five hundred calories, or a full pound's worth. If you combine your walking with a diet which reduces your caloric intake by a further three hundred calories a day, you will create an additional calorie deficit of over seven thousand calories—or a total weight loss of three pounds. That may not sound like much, but it's about a pound a week, and most doctors emphasize that a slow but steady weight loss is the safest way both to lose pounds and to keep them off. Furthermore, the exercise will make you look slimmer than the scales show, by toning and firming your body.

A final myth about diet and exercise is that weight can be lost through passive means, such as massage, tight wrapping, or sweating. This, too, is absolutely false. Massages feel wonderful, and they may temporarily improve the flexibility of your joints, but they simply cannot help you lose weight. The only way to lose weight is to use up more calories than you are taking in, and the only person using up a significant amount of calories during a massage is the masseur.

Similarly, tight wrapping, whether with special belts, fabrics, or good old Saran Wrap, won't help you lose weight. What may happen if you tightly wrap an area such as the abdomen for several hours is that the fat is compressed, and so for a while you will both measure and look slimmer. But eventually the fat is going to resume its normal shape, and you will be no thinner than you were before. And as for sweating off excess weight, while I admit it's a cheering picture to imagine fat globules disappearing into the mist of a steam room, the fact is that you don't sweat fat; you sweat water. After a steam or sauna session, you may indeed weigh less—but that loss was all water, and it will all come back as soon as you drink enough to replace it.

So once again, we come back to exercise combined with a diet as the best and most realistic way to lose weight.

How Exercise Can Help You Lose Weight

How does regular exercise help you lose weight? It does it in several ways, and an understanding of these ways can help you to plan your own exercise program to maximize weight loss.

In the first place, as I previously mentioned, regular vigorous exercise depresses the appetite. This is because your blood-sugar level, one of the cues that signals hunger, is raised during and for a significant period of time after exercise. Furthermore, after exercise the blood supply essential for good digestion is still mainly in your muscles, where it is washing away the waste products of exercise and delivering oxygen to your tissues. Your stomach just isn't ready to go to work after a workout. You can prove this to yourself the next time you feel weak and "starved"—instead of eating something, go for a long, brisk walk. (Don't try this, of course, if you have hypoglycemia or diabetes.) Within a very short period of time, you will quite simply no longer be hungry. And if you don't wait too long to eat after you return home, you will probably be satisfied with something very light, such as yogurt or a salad.

Since the appetite-depressing effect of exercise can make it much easier to stick to a reducing diet, you might try to schedule your exercise session before your biggest meal of the day, then make that meal a light one. The only will power you will need is in avoiding the psychological trap of telling yourself you deserve a big meal because of all the hard work you just did.

The second way in which exercise aids in weight loss is that, as noted, the exercise itself uses up calories. Even if you don't diet at all, increasing the level of your physical activity will reduce your weight over a period of time. If you have a great deal of weight to lose, of course, the amount may not be significant, but losses of ten to fifteen pounds a year are common in people who take up jogging or swimming on a regular basis. And I know from my own experience that whenever I increase my level of exercise, I start losing weight, whether I plan to or not. (In fact, I am now as thin as I ever want to be, and anytime I take up a new physical activity, I have to consciously increase my food intake to keep my weight from going even lower: I simply can't afford to buy a whole new wardrobe!)

Finally, exercise can help you lose weight by making you more aware of your body and its needs. It has been shown that many overweight people respond to external cues rather than to true internal hunger. If you walk into a room and see a big plate of home-made doughnuts on the table, your mind may tell you, "I'm hungry!" even though your body doesn't really want any food at the moment. You can start to over-come this problem by learning to listen to your body and what it is really telling you.

The idea of listening to your body is not as mystical as it sounds. As thousands of devotees of physical activity can attest, regular exercise seems somehow to normalize your body. After all, when humans were evolving, vigorous daily exercise was essential for sur-vival; just because there's no economic reason for most of us to get regular exercise today doesn't mean that our bodies have outgrown their need for it. Some studies have shown that human infants, given a wide selection of foods and left to make their own choices, spontaneously select a combination of foods that gives them the proper balance of nutrients. And most young children, if they are not psychological captives of tele-vision, will ordinarily spend a great part of their day in quite vigorous and seemingly unending physical activity. For many of us, that seemingly innate wis-dom disappears as we are growing up; left to our own devices and given a free choice as adults, we will spend far too much of our time sitting around eating potato chips and drinking soda.

Regular exercise, by putting you in touch with your body, can help you relearn the wisdom that is within you. In my own case, I eat less now than I used to before I became fitness-conscious. This is not because I am denying myself, but simply because I want less food—and, just as important, I *realize* that I want less food. Furthermore, the food I eat tends to be more natural and less of the junk variety. (I guess I'm just not listening those times my body tells me it doesn't really want beer and pizza.) I have no proof of this, but I believe that because I exercise regularly my body is now living the way it was meant to live, and that my innate "body wisdom" has in some way been switched back on.

What exercise should you choose to help you lose weight? Well, any activity is better than none. To be perfectly honest, although the Basic Strength Program does burn some calories, since it is performed only three times a week, it is not going to put a significant dent in your calorie budget. Remember, the main purpose of the program is to develop muscle tone, strength, and endurance. The best form of exercise for a steady weight loss is one you perform at least four times a week for twenty minutes to half an hour. Aerobic exercises—jogging, swimming, walking, cycling—are the best. A calisthenics program which includes continuous rhythmic exercises involving your largest muscle groups will also burn many calories.

If you are not now doing an aerobic program and don't feel you are ready for such vigorous exercise yet, try the following routine for maximum weight loss with minimum discomfort: diet; the Basic Strength Program three times a week; and a half-hour walk a day, every day. This plan should create a gradual but steady loss of weight. Best of all, if you conscientiously work on the Basic Strength Program, not only will you reshape your slimmer figure, you may avoid many of the problems that often accompany weight loss, such as saggy skin and stretch marks.

How Weight Training Can Help Reshape Your Figure

You may have heard that weight training can result in weight gain; in fact, in those ads in the men's magazines aimed at ninety-five-pound weaklings, adding bulk (weight) is often the explicit goal of weight training. And indeed this does happen—for people who train specifically in order to gain weight. As I've stated before, muscle weighs more than fat, so if you add muscle mass to your body, you may add pounds as well.

But this is more true for men than for women; because women are not capable of developing large amounts of muscle mass, they are less likely to gain weight while becoming stronger. And again, as excess fat on your body is replaced by muscle, you will be much slimmer even if your scales don't show any weight loss.

Different techniques are employed in weight training when weight gain is desired. For maximum gain in muscle bulk, a low number of reps with a very high resistance (weight) is used; for slimming, a higher number of reps with less weight is best. For the exercises in the Basic Strength Program, none of the weights used is heavy enough to add much muscle mass, only to increase muscular strength and endurance, so unless you decide to greatly increase the amount of weight you are using, you don't need to worry about gaining weight while on the program.

The Basic Strength Program will, however, help you reshape your figure until it approaches the ideal *for you.* I emphasize *for you*, because there is no way every woman can achieve a figure considered perfect or ideal by everyone; we simply aren't all built alike. But unless you are going to be bitterly disappointed if you don't end up looking like Farrah Fawcett-Majors, you should see a pleasing change in your proportions and in the firmness of areas all over your body as you progress with the Basic Strength Program.

Bear in mind that a high number of reps done with light weights will help slim any area you are particularly concerned about. A middle-aged woman I know decided to try my program because she was tired of having flabby upper arms. Although she did not particularly work on increasing her strength (in fact, she didn't progress beyond one-pound weights for any of the exercises), she did increase the number of reps and sets consistently. After only eight weeks on the program, Jane was delighted to report that she had lost half an inch from each of her upper arms and that her arms themselves looked much smoother and firmer. In addition, although she had not concentrated on those areas, she had lost another half inch from her waist, and half an inch from her upper thighs. Another friend who tried my program tells me that at long last she is beginning to lose the "saddlebags" of fat on her upper thighs which years of dieting, yoga, and floor rolls had refused to budge.

Special Foods for Exercising

Although attitudes are changing, there is a widespread belief that an athlete must eat more food than a nonathlete and that the food she eats has to be of the steak-and-potatoes variety. Like so many other ideas about diet and exercise, this is a myth.

Protein is often referred to as the basic building block of the body, and all of us need a certain amount of this nutrient in our food. But there is no evidence that an athlete needs any more protein than anyone else. Your body, remember, was designed to be active; if you exercise vigorously and regularly and don't force yourself to eat a lot, you may become skinny— but you certainly won't suffer from malnutrition, assuming you eat a well-balanced diet including all the basic food groups. Protein is supplied in greater and lesser amounts by the foods in each of these groups (even vegetables and fruits contain some protein), so there's no need to add any extra meat of any sort. In fact, many athletes I know are vegetarians; I personally haven't eaten any flesh other than fish for four years, and I've never felt better. A survey of top distance runners in the country showed that the majority of these athletes eat diets which consist largely of fresh vegetables and fruit, plus a very small amount of meat and other animal products.

Supplements and Athletic Beverages

A health-food store owner once told me that the richest natural source of vitamin B is middle-class urine. Be that as it may, like many other fitness-conscious people, I take a wide variety of supplements. My theory is that it can't hurt and might help, but of course I can't suggest or prescribe any particular supplements. The vitamins most often taken by athletes I know are C and E; in your own case, you should of course always check with your doctor before adding anything unusual to your diet.

As for special athletic beverages, there are several on the market, but these are designed mainly to replace minerals lost in sweat by people who perform a great deal of physical activity, such as running long distances or playing several sets of tennis. Since the Basic Strength Program takes only fifteen minutes or so, you won't produce enough sweat to deplete these minerals.

Finally, it is often thought that an athlete should eat more iron, the main component of the oxygen-carrying part of the blood. There is no evidence that strenuous activity increases your need for this important mineral, but it is true that many women are chronically iron-deficient because of blood loss during menstruation. It makes sense, then, to include iron-containing foods in your diet: These include organ meats, such as liver; egg yolks; and green leafy vegetables.

10

STRENGTH IN YOUR LIFE

Weak No More, My Lady

Developing muscular fitness is like taking a journey to an unknown land—the land in this case being your own body. As you continue to build strength, you will probably become increasingly aware of aspects of your physical self that you have never been in touch with. For example, when you skip workouts for several days, your body will let you know it, because the muscles will rebel against inactivity. They will ask you to return to your exercise regimen with a vague, not-quite-aching feeling, similar to that signal sent out in childhood by a loose tooth: a signal that was not quite pain but clearly said, "Wiggle me." In the same way, your muscles will demand that you continue to exercise by sending out subtle signals that say, "Work me."

You may find yourself spontaneously becoming more active in response to these new muscular signals. Suddenly you are walking instead of taking the bus, carrying packages home from a department store instead of having them sent, rearranging your living room instead of waiting till the next time you move. You may even get carried away with your new-found strength and start to perform physical feats that you aren't really prepared for or don't know how to do correctly.

This happened to me a few weeks after I had begun my strength-building program. One day a friend who had laughed at my "pumping tomato juice" offered to lend me a fairly heavy typing table. He lived several blocks away, and I had originally decided to take the table home in a taxi. But when he asked me whether I needed help getting it home, the show-off in me took over. "No, thanks," I said. "I can carry it. It's only a few blocks."

Ignoring his skeptical look, I confidently picked up the table and began walking downtown, my strong right arm around the table, my body bent to the right in response to the weight. Although the table was heavy, the only real discomfort I felt was in my hands, where the edge of the table was cutting. Twice on the way home I stopped and switched the table to the other side, and finally arrived home in triumph, not even tired. I was woman, I was strong, and I could do anything.

The next morning I woke up with aching shoulders and a pain in my lower back. Although the aches and pains weren't debilitating, I found it almost impossible to get through my regular exercise routine that afternoon, and it took me nearly a week to recover my former level of well-being. The moral of this story is twofold: I should not have assumed that I could carry a heavy weight a long distance when I had not had practice carrying weights even short distances, and I probably should not have carried a weight any distance without some knowledge of the mechanics of the correct way to carry things.

One reason that correct technique is so important in the exercise of weight lifting is that our bodies are like machines, designed to work according to certain mechanical principles. But most of us, and that includes men as well as women, don't know these principles and have a tendency to do what seems natural: reach out and grab, bend with the weight, and lift only from the upper body—when actually the powerful leg muscles should be involved.

Incorrect lifting and carrying not only can cause injury; they can make the performance of any task harder and more fatiguing. Now that you are stronger, you will find yourself able to do things that were formerly difficult or impossible for you, but to keep them from becoming injurious or even harder to do, here are some tips on how to approach those daily activities in which strength and proper mechanical performance are important.

Pushing and Pulling

It's eight P.M., you're alone in the house, your boss is due for dinner, and your cat has just knocked your wire whisk behind a heavy kitchen cabinet. You need the whisk, but how can you move the cabinet all by yourself?

Well, possibly you can't. It may be too heavy for you, and if that is the case, give up on the hollandaise and wait until you can get help. But you can at least give it a try.

Whenever you have to move a very heavy object, it will be easier to budge if you remember one basic rule: broaden your base of support. This means, simply, to spread your legs and bend at the knees. This brings your center of gravity (balance point) lower and provides stability, while allowing you to apply strength from your powerful leg muscles. It may seem strange to think of pushing from the legs, but this is the most effective way to use your body's strength.

The stronger and firmer your upper-body muscles are, the more directly you can transfer the force produced by your legs to the object you need to move.

When approaching a heavy object, stand slightly away from it, so you can lean your body toward it while you push. Then apply slow, steady pressure, keeping your knees bent and your back straight.

When pulling, the same principles apply: feet apart, knees slightly bent, back straight. Avoid bending your trunk backwards, as this can put excessive strain on your lower-back muscles.

Lifting

This activity is performed dozens of times a day, from simply lifting a pencil off your desk to retrieving a dropped pocketbook. Where many women run into trouble (such as back injury) is in trying to lift heavy objects the same way as lightweight ones.

Suppose you are landscaping your terrace, and you need to move some heavy flowerpots from one area to another. The usual tendency is to bend over from the waist and simply pick the flowerpot up, using your arms to hold it and your back to lift it. An easier and safer way to pick up the pot is to stand above it, your legs apart and one foot slightly in front of the other, and bend from the knees. Keep your back straight while you grasp the pot (remember, the lower back's main function is to straighten your trunk), and straighten your knees, letting your powerful thigh muscles do as much of the work of lifting as possible. The heavier or bulkier the object, the more important it is to lift it with the thighs. Furthermore, people who have back trouble should *always* lift by stooping rather than bending, no matter how light or small the object is.

To lift a heavy object from a table, the same principles apply: your legs should be spread, with one foot slightly in front of the other. Get as close to the object as possible. Keep your knees flexed and your back straight, to take the strain off your lower back.

In lifting a heavy object from one side (such as a large, bulky suitcase), first spread your legs and place one foot in front of the other. Get as close to the object as you can, bend your knees, and use as much of the power of your thighs to lift as you can. Keep your back straight as you lift—avoid a tendency to let your body bend to the side.

Another lift that we all perform occasionally involves taking a heavy object down from a high shelf. Those who have small city-apartment kitchens are often faced with this problem: the heavier, less-used pots and pans are sometimes stored out of the way on very high shelves. When removing an object of any weight from such a shelf or from the top of a closet, first broaden your base of support by spreading your feet, one foot slightly in front of the other. Stand fairly close to the shelf but not directly underneath it, because the weight can cause your upper body to fall suddenly backwards, straining your lower back.

The principles involved in lifting loose objects apply to other kinds of lifting as well. In opening a stuck window, for example, you proceed as you would for lifting a heavy object from a table. Approach it feet apart, one in front of the other, knees bent. Grasp the window sash, then straighten your knees as you push upward.

In any lifting task, it's extremely important to keep your hips *under your trunk* while you straighten your legs—don't let your hips push out behind you. If you find that an object does not budge as you begin to straighten your legs, give up and wait until you can get help; otherwise, you could strain your back.

Carrying

The principles for carrying objects are the same as for lifting: You want to maintain the greatest stability possible without putting any unusual strain on your body, especially your back.

When carrying something in front, such as a heavy sack of groceries, keep the object as close to your body as possible. Your back should be straight—if the object is so heavy that you find your trunk bending backward, that object is too heavy for you and you should either make two trips or try to find help.

An efficient position for holding bulky objects is similar to the way you hold a baby—cradle the object with one arm while supporting it from the bottom with the other.

When carrying a heavy object at your side, some people tend to lean toward the weight. Not only can this cause strain (it was what caused my back pain the time I carried a typewriter table home), it is fatiguing and inefficient. The next time you have to lug a heavy suitcase around an airport terminal, keep your back straight and lean your whole body away from the suitcase. You'll find that it will be much easier to carry this way. If the suitcase is very heavy, stop and change hands from time to time.

Good Posture: How to Carry Yourself

"Stand up straight!" "Hold your stomach in!" "Watch your posture!" Do these admonitions sound familiar? Unless you are quite unusual, you heard them often while you were growing up—and if you're anything like me, you ignored them.

When I was a teenager, the idea of good posture

became something of a joke in my high school. For some reason, the Girls' P.E. Department issued an annual award to the girl who was judged by the gym teachers to have the best posture in the school. The girl who won had her picture and name posted on bulletin boards around the school, and she was given the title of "Miss Perfect Posture." I remember the year a close friend of mine who was naturally shy was voted Miss Perfect Posture. For months thereafter poor Paula was taunted and called Miss P-P by almost everyone, and she once jokingly told me that she envied my slouch!

Even with "Miss P-P" as a model, though, most of the girls in my high school were only minimally aware of the importance of good posture. After all, none of us really understood the criteria by which the winner was chosen. And even had we understood them, none of us was given remedial exercises to improve our own posture. What was good posture anyway? Paula looked great, but she was the kind of girl who would have looked great crawling on all fours—and there were other girls who looked just as great but who didn't stand up nearly as straight as she did.

So what, then, is good posture, and why is it important?

Quite simply, posture is the way you carry your body (a dictionary synonym, in fact, is "carriage"). "Good posture" and "bad posture" are not value judgments; they merely reflect the efficiency with which a person uses her muscles to maintain the alignment of her skeleton. Essentially, posture can be thought of as more of an engineering matter than a biological one. Good posture is really just an alignment of the bones that does not put uneven stress on any parts of the body; it is an efficient balance of the body in which the muscles that counteract gravity can perform their work of keeping the body upright with a minimum amount of work, and in which all motions can be performed most economically and with the least waste of energy. Although certain principles apply to all good posture, the most efficient carriage will vary from person to person, depending on build and weight; it can also change over the lifetime of a person. A woman who is seven months pregnant will carry herself in a very different manner from a woman who is not pregnant, and yet each might be practicing what is considered good posture.

But if good posture is so natural, why don't more people have perfect posture? The main reason, surprisingly enough, is habit. Your body adapts to habit. If you are in the habit of smoking a pack of cigarettes a day, the smoking of the cigarettes becomes an almost unconscious thing on your part. Your body adapts as well as it can by, among other things, producing more mucus to expel the poisonous substances in the smoke from your lungs. If you work on an assembly line all day, your body will similarly adapt by strengthening the front muscles, which are used in the work, while your back muscles will stretch out to accommodate the position you stand in. Because these back muscles are not being used in the work, they will also become weaker, relatively, than the muscles in front. Eventually, this imbalance will become a part of your carriage, whether you are working or not. Similarly, if you spend a lot of time at cocktail parties and customarily stand with a drink in one hand and your body balanced on one hip, gradually the muscles on the side you lean toward will shorten, while those on the other side will lengthen. And again, these changes will eventually be reflected in your everyday posture.

If any such habit continues for a long period of time, it becomes very difficult to *consciously* change your posture, because the muscular imbalance has become too great. A more correct, efficient posture will feel uncomfortable, so you will tend to continue the bad postural habits in all areas of your life, which will reinforce the imbalance, and so on in a truly vicious circle.

In some extreme cases, postural imbalance can lead to actual structural deformities, such as a distorted spine or the condition known as "dowager's hump," in which the chest muscles become shorter and shorter as the back muscles become weaker and weaker, until the entire upper-back structure is pulled forward into a hunched, stooped position. Even though men can develop this condition, it is called dowager's hump because it is most common in elderly women who have suffered from extremely weak upper-back muscles their whole lives.

It should be clear by now that posture is dynamic: that is, "good posture" does not apply just to standing, but to walking, sitting, running, indeed to any activity.

Although very few people have posture poor enough to be noticeably deforming, the majority of Americans have one or more bad habits that can affect the way they feel as well as the way they look. The good news is that it's not difficult to change these postural imbalances.

Since your own posture is largely a result of habit, you can go a long way toward improving it just by changing the bad habits: try not to stand with your weight on one hip; try not to slouch; keep your back straight when working at a desk, and so on. But since it may be difficult or even painful to get into new and better habits while you still maintain muscle imbalances, it can be helpful to concentrate on strength-building exercises for your weaker muscles while working on stretching the stronger, tighter muscles.

The small amount of effort expended in improving your posture will give you many positive results. As your posture improves, so does your figure, for you tend to look slimmer (nothing is sagging) and stand taller. Just as important, you will find that with better posture you will feel less fatigue, both in your daily activities and when standing or walking, because the muscles used in these activities will have to do less work to overcome the imbalances that formerly restricted their movements. It will even become easier to do your strength-building exercises and to play sports, as each muscle is allowed to perform with a maximum of economy, efficiency, and range of motion. Finally, good posture can reduce the chances of certain types of injuries, such as a slipped disc.

You and Your Posture

How good is your own posture? The chances are that you have at least some postural imbalance, although it may not be readily noticeable. The easiest way to find out whether you have any very obvious problem is to ask your friends and relatives or your doctor. They may have noticed a tendency toward stooped shoulders or a curved lower back and said nothing about it, out of kindness. Or perhaps you're the kind of person who is still being told to stand up straight or sit up straight.

Although self-examination can be depressing, you can get a good idea of your own postural weaknesses by looking in a mirror while you are naked. A three-way mirror is best, but it's not absolutely necessary.

First, face the mirror and "let it all hang out." No cheating—if you don't usually hold in your stomach, don't do so now. These are the things to look for: is one shoulder higher than the other, or does one shoulder slope downward more than the other? If so, look at the hip area on the same side as the lower shoulder;

even if it isn't readily apparent, that hip is probably higher than the other.

Now turn to the side. Is your head carried noticeably forward? Do your shoulders tend to droop to the front? Is the upper part of your back curved markedly forward rather than relatively straight? These problems tend to go together and are usually the result of spending a lot of time working at a desk or on an assembly line. Finally, check your lower back. Does it curve markedly to the front, allowing your abdomen to protrude?

Each of the problems above can be improved through a combination of proper exercise and the change of a few habits in your daily life. However, if you have any postural imbalance to a really noticeable degree, or if you have severe pain in any area of your back, check with an orthopedist before trying any corrective exercises on your own.

To check for good standing posture, stand with your back to a wall, your feet comfortably apart with toes pointing ahead, your heels three to four inches from the wall and your shoulders lightly touching it. Now check each part of your body, concentrating on how it feels. If you are standing in good postural balance, your head should be directly above your shoulders (not tilted forward or back), with your chin held level. Your back should be straight, your knees relaxed. Your shoulders too should be relaxed, not pulled upward, forward, or back. If this posture feels strange to you, try practicing it frequently, until it becomes and feels natural.

Below are some suggestions for dealing with common postural imbalances. Bear in mind that the solution to the problem, whatever it is, primarily involves strengthening the weaker muscles while stretching the opposing, stronger muscles.

One Shoulder Lower Than the Other

This fairly common postural problem is often caused, as previously mentioned, by a tendency to stand with your weight balanced on one hip. A contributing habit is that of always carrying objects on one side of your body. As a result of these habits, the muscles on the favored side tend to become stronger and therefore shorter, while the muscles on the other side become progressively weaker.

A good exercise for stretching the muscles on your weaker side is a modification of the side stretcher warmup (p. 62). When using this exercise for posture correction, exaggerate the part of the stretch toward your weaker side. So, if your right shoulder is lower, stretch to the right as always for the warmup, but then stretch farther to the left. Hold the stretch to the left for a count of ten; repeat ten to twenty times.

To develop strength on the weaker side, it can help in the Basic Strength Program to do an extra set of shoulder and arm exercises with the weaker side only. Do it as part of your regular exercise routine: after you finish your regular sets for these muscles in the Basic or Maintenance program, add another set for your weaker side only.

From now on, practice carrying things on the weak side—from your pocketbook to bags of groceries. If your weak side is not strong enough yet to carry a heavy bag of purchases, ask for two bags and hold the heaviest one you can carry in the weak arm while carrying the lighter one with your strong side. And of course avoid standing with all your weight on one hip.

Round Shoulders

In the case of round or forward-sloping shoulders, the muscular imbalance is one of too-strong chest muscles opposed by too-weak back muscles. The solution is to strengthen the back muscles, and one of the best exercises for this is the bent-over row (Substitute Exercise IIIF, p. 97). In addition, you can increase the sets and/or reps of your regular upper-back exercises.

If you spend a lot of time working at a desk, you can help to break bad sitting habits by taking frequent rest breaks. During the break, stand up, walk around, rotate your shoulders from front to back. Finish with the neck relaxer:

NECK RELAXER

Sitting or standing in a comfortable position, let your head drop back until you are looking up at the ceiling. Now slowly roll your head to the right until it is resting on your right shoulder, hold a moment, then roll your head until it is hanging down in front. Again hold, then roll your head to the left until it is resting on your left shoulder. Hold a moment, and roll your head to the back again. Hold, then repeat the sequence, this time rolling your head in the opposite direction. Repeat the entire sequence one more time.

A couple of rounds of the neck relaxer not only can help break bad habits that are contributing to your round shoulders, but will also help to relieve tension in the shoulders and the back of the neck.

Another excellent exercise to relieve tension and promote relaxation in the entire upper-body area is the passive stretch, which consists of simply hanging from a high bar, your feet not touching the ground. This is obviously not practical for most women, but if you belong to a gym, try this at the end of your regular workout.

Dowager's Hump

Dowager's hump and round shoulders are closely related, resulting from the same muscular imbalance, and the exercises for one can be used to help the other.

Once you have actually developed the extreme form of this condition, it is difficult to eliminate it, but it can be helped, and you can prevent it from becoming worse by doing the following exercises.

First, as for round shoulders, do the bent-over row and other upper-back exercises. Another good exercise for strengthening the upper back is the upright row.

UPRIGHT ROW

Start: Stand comfortably, weights in each hand held in an overhand grip (your palms facing your body), your arms hanging so that your hands are in front of your thighs.

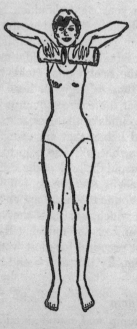

Upright row

Move: Bend your arms, slowly raising both weights to the level of your chin, keeping your hands close together, knuckles facing each other. Your elbows should be out and above your hands throughout the lift. Hold a moment, lower the weights, then repeat. Be sure to keep your back straight when performing this exercise; don't bend from the waist either forward or backward.

Suggested starting weight: Three to five pounds. Start with two consecutive sets of six to eight reps each, build to two sets of twelve, then move on to a heavier weight at two sets of six reps each.

Goal: Two sets of twelve reps, each with a weight of five to eight pounds.

In addition to strengthening the upper back, you also want to stretch the muscles of the chest and the front of the neck. For the latter, try the neck relaxer described above. To stretch your chest muscles, do the arm fling (Exercise IIIA in the Basic Strength Program, p. 71). Start with ten reps of each fling, build to as many as thirty or forty of each. The passive stretch (p. 159), if you have access to a high bar, is also excellent.

Swayback

This condition is quite common in women who have lost the tone and strength of their abdominal muscles. As the lower-back and leg muscles are relatively stronger in these women, the lower back's natural curve tends to become exaggerated, resulting in swayback and a protruding abdomen.

To improve this condition, you should stretch your lower-back and back leg muscles, while improving abdominal strength.

One of the best ways to stretch your lower back is to spend some extra time on your regular warmup exercises, particularly the back stretcher (p. 61). Remember as you perform these to *hold* the stretch—no bouncing or jerking.

To strengthen your abdominals, of course, do more situps. If you have been doing the half-situp (Exercise IXA, p. 83), perhaps now is the time to try one of the more advanced positions, the modified situp or the chair situp (Exercises IX C&B, p. 84). Even if you can do only one at first, gradually build until you can do twenty to thirty.

When performing any exercises for specific postural problems, you will get best results if you do them every other day, though you will notice some improvement if you simply incorporate them into your regular workout. All stretching exercises can be performed as part of your regular warmup. The strength-building exercises can become part of your regular routine also, though you should try to increase the number of reps and/or sets. And remember to perform them in the correct order, by muscle group.

Even if you routinely and faithfully perform exercises to improve your posture, bear in mind that they won't help much unless you also break some of the bad habits that have caused the disturbances. Some of these habits are so ingrained that it will take a great deal of conscious effort to change them—but it will be worth it. And sometimes simply changing your physical environment will do the trick.

For example, if you are an executive, a student, or any sort of office worker, you probably spend a lot of time at a desk. It's easy to get into the habit of hunching over your work, and this is especially true when you are working at a desk or table that is too low. Any surface that you work on should be sufficiently high that you can work without having to bend over, whether you are standing or sitting.

In most cases, this is easier said than done. Sinks, desks, and tables are all built at standard heights, which would be fine if all of us were also made in standard heights; but since we aren't, what may be an ideal kitchen counter for one woman is a postural booby trap for another. Even if you can't get new furniture or kitchen fixtures, though, you can sometimes modify them—by sitting in a lower chair, for example, or chopping carrots while seated at the table rather than standing at the sink. If your desk if too low for you to type on, try placing your typewriter on top of a telephone book while you work. If your desk is too high, try placing yourself on the telephone book. A man I used to work with always did his typing standing up, with his typewriter on a bookshelf, because it was the only position he could work in without fatigue. An adjustable ironing board is an excellent investment; not only can it be set for various heights while you are ironing, but you can use it for other tasks where a level surface is required—writing, sewing, even typing.

If you must work at a desk or counter that is the wrong height for you, remember to take frequent rest breaks and perform some of the loosening exercises suggested for round shoulders. Also, when working at a desk of any type, whenever you need to bring your eyes closer to the work, do it by bending your whole upper body forward from the *hips*.

When sitting in a chair, a general rule for ensuring good posture is to sit in *all of the chair*. If you sit forward, for example, there will be a tendency to let your back slump against the back of the chair; if you sit so that your back is supported by the chair, it will be easier to keep your spine straight. Sitting on the floor is more tiring than sitting in a chair, because the back is unsupported. If you are fairly flexible, you will probably find cross-legged or kneeling positions most comfortable, because these positions will enable you to keep your back straight. Another comfortable position for many people is one in which both legs are folded to one side, but if you sit this way, change sides from time to time. Finally, if you must sit with your legs stretched out in front of you, support your back by leaning against a wall or a stationary piece of furniture.

People who have to stand a lot not only can develop postural problems, they can also develop circulatory problems in their legs. Whenever you must stand for long periods, it's important to move around as much as possible, even if it means taking small steps in place. To avoid fatigue and the tendency to balance your weight on one hip, try standing as follows: stand with your legs comfortably apart, one foot slightly in front of the other. Keep your back straight, and shift your weight from one foot to the other whenever you start to feel tired. This sounds too simple to be effective, but it really works. The key, of course, is keeping one foot in front of the other; most of us have a tendency to stand with our feet even, which is an inefficient position for maintaining balance.

There are many other habits in our daily life which contribute to postural imbalances. Even the position in which you sleep is considered important. Most experts advise sleeping on your side, but I have never understood how one can consciously change the position in which she sleeps. If you try always to fall asleep on your side, perhaps it will become a habit for you.

The best way to ensure good posture and daily comfort, of course, is to become aware of your body and how you are holding it. I'm still working on some of my postural problems, and I've found that since I started doing exercises for my stooped shoulders, they are getting less stooped, and I'm far more conscious of how I sit and stand. With this new consciousness, it seems easier and more natural to carry myself correctly; for you, too, good posture can mean looking and feeling better all day long.

PART II

11

GETTING STRONG FOR SPORTS

Women, Sports, and Society

You can get a very revealing idea of the attitude of society toward women in sports by taking the following simple quiz: in five minutes or less, list as many famous male and female athletes as you can—but no more than one of each sex for the same sport. Ready? Go.

How many did you list? Chances are you had no trouble thinking of the names of men in many different sports—Julius Erving, Péle, Hank Aaron, Joe Namath, Frank Shorter, Mark Spitz, Bruce Jenner, Muhammad Ali, Arnold Palmer, and on and on. In fact, name just about any sport in the world, and you've probably at least heard of one male athlete who competes in it. But what about the women's list? Well, you probably first thought of Billie Jean King, Nadia Comaneci, Miki Gorman, Dorothy Hamill, perhaps Janie Blalock or Diana Nyad. But when you try to expand the list, it becomes more difficult, because, although women participate in nearly as many sports as men do, few of us make the same kind of name in them as men. In fact, it is only in a very few sports that women receive any general publicity at all. If the quiz were altered so that you could list several women athletes in each sport, your list would undoubtedly be top-heavy with the names of tennis champions, gymnasts, and figure skaters.

The fact is that women as athletes are only now beginning to come into the public consciousness. In an article for *WomenSports* magazine, Molly Tyson described the results of a questionnaire given to Long Island schoolchildren. The children were first asked to list ten male and ten female athletes. On an average, the girls were able to identify 6.1 men and 4.6 women, while the boys named 7.5 men and 2.3 women. Of the top three women named by the children, the list was headed by Dorothy Hamill, a great athlete, but one who performs in a sport which has long been considered mainly for women; she was followed by Nadia Comaneci, who again is in a sport associated in the popular mind with women, and Chris Evert, who has received wide publicity for her charm and "femininity" as well as for her considerable sports achievements.

The very idea of a woman soccer player, baseball player, basketball forward, or boxer is still foreign and frightening to the majority of Americans. The New York State Boxing Commission still refuses to license female boxers, although professional women boxers compete in bouts in neighboring states.

Even in less "masculine" sports, women have been excluded. As recently as ten years ago, Kathrine Switzer was physically assaulted by an official attempting to throw her out of the Boston Marathon, an all-male race at the time, because she had registered under the "fraudulent" name of K. Switzer. Afterward, she was suspended by the AAU (which sanctions sports activities in this country) for, among other things, "running with men" and "running without a chaperone." This sounds like something that might have happened in Victorian times, but that history-making marathon was run in 1967!

Why were women barred from Boston (and most other long-distance races)? Because it was assumed by the male organizers of these events that women were unable to compete in them and did not want to compete in them. This attitude prevailed—and in many cases still prevails—for most other sports. Even when growing numbers of women athletes proved that both these assumptions were not true, conventional sports medicine provided yet another rationalization for excluding women from sports: physical activity could be harmful to their health.

At the time Kathrine Switzer was growing up (the fifties and sixties), young female athletes were often told by coaches and doctors that if they didn't ease up on sports activities they might permanently injure their reproductive organs. "It was a very scary idea," Switzer says now. "I had to seriously consider—what am I doing to my body? Do I have to choose between sports and having a baby someday?" Defying the stern words of warning, Switzer continued to remain active in sports: aside from running, she was on her high school's varsity field-hockey team, and she played such other sports as tennis and golf. "Instinctively, I just felt I couldn't be harming myself," she says. "Physical activity felt too good to be as bad as they were saying."

Today, of course, we know that physical activity is more likely to make a person of either sex healthier and less subject to diseases of any system. And yet many of the old taboos and fears about women playing sports still apply. Maybe it's all right for women to play tennis and run, the argument goes, but they mustn't be allowed to play vigorous contact sports, because they might become injured. True enough. Women who play such contact sports as football and basketball do become injured—at least more often than men do. But a primary reason for most of these injuries is that women have not developed their physical strength to the same extent as men. Also, most women athletes are not as well trained as most men athletes. Furthermore, with few exceptions, there is no protective equipment, such as shin guards and helmets, made in women's sizes.

Shin guards and helmets are so basic to men's sports that they are almost taken for granted; in women's sports nothing is taken for granted. I'm always amused when I hear a male jock talk about how dangerous it is for a woman to play a sport like football or baseball, because she might injure her breasts. The obvious solution, of course, is to design protective equipment for the breasts. (Such equipment does exist, but because it is so new, many coaches feel it isn't as well designed as it could be for maximum comfort and protection.) Whenever I hear this argument advanced against women's full participation in sports, I can't help thinking about the area where male athletes are most vulnerable. Men are often hit in the groin in contact and even non-contact sports, and I've been assured by men of my acquaintance that it hurts even with the protection of armored jockstraps. Furthermore, because of their body structure, men are far more vulnerable to hernias when performing violent activity. I sometimes feel that perhaps we would all be better off if women, whose reproductive organs are well protected deep inside their bodies, engaged in the more vigorous sports and left the quieter pursuits to men.

Once it has been shown that women *can* play all sports, and once they are provided with protective equipment, there remains one last formidable barrier to overcome before full participation for women will be a reality. That barrier is, I think, best demonstrated by the hysteria generated in recent years by decisions to open Little League baseball teams to girls as well as boys. From the reactions of many Little League managers and the players' parents, you would think the towns involved had been facing imminent invasion by Mongol hordes at the very least. And was it because some little girls wanted to play ball? No, far worse: because some little girls wanted to play ball *with little boys*.

I believe that this fear of coeducational sports is a direct response to the—admittedly weakening—influence of male chauvinism on American life. "All right," the reasoning must go, "the courts have forced us to let women into the board room, but by God there's no way we're going to allow them on the football field." This attitude is still a dominant one. In that questionnaire in which schoolchildren were asked to name sports heroes, they were also asked whether boys and girls should be allowed to play on the same teams. A majority of the boys (fifty-five percent) resoundingly said no, while the girls even more resoundingly (eighty-two percent) said yes. The nay-saying boys gave such explanations for their attitudes as "girls are bad luck" and "girls get in the way and can't even throw."

This male idea that "girls are bad luck" is ultimately what's behind all of the attempts to keep women second-class citizens in sports. Even with Title IX, most school systems and colleges are dragging their feet about allowing girls and women the full access to physical education and sports that they are now legally entitled to. Not that I believe there is a conscious conspiracy here, of course; and many male athletes, such as Dr. Stauffer and Dr. Peterson, are champions of women's rights in every area, from the economic to the athletic. Still, behind such excuses as "women's sports generate less money" to justify less than full compliance with Title IX lurks this very frightening thought: if women are allowed to participate fully in sports, they might someday be able to play as well as men. And if *that* happens . . . how can they be stopped from actually playing with men?

I don't mean to imply that there aren't differences in the potential for athletic performance between men and women. Of course there are—differences based on our skeletal structure, our relative size, and other inherent physiological factors. But because women have been virtually barred from participation in sports for so long, no one really knows just what women's physical potential really is (though in a few sports in which women have long competed, we are beginning to get an idea of this potential—in the perfect performances of Nadia Comaneci and the stunning marathon swims of Diana Nyad).

In general terms, the physical differences between men and women are as follows: women have greater coordination, flexibility and balance, while men, who have a higher proportion of muscle mass to body weight, are stronger, faster, and more powerful. Although men have long been considered to have more endurance as well, growing evidence suggests that women's greater reserves of fat may actually give them the advantage in endurance, particularly in such grueling events as ultramarathoning (racing more than twenty-six miles) and marathon swimming. Still, as a recent article in *Search* magazine pointed out, there is a wider range of differences among athletes of the same sex than there is between men and women.

Not surprisingly, most of the moneymaking professional sports emphasize the areas in which men have the advantage—football, with its stress on physical size, speed, and raw power; basketball, with its emphasis on height and speed; and hockey, with its emphasis on physical violence. Certainly it would be difficult for a female athlete, no matter how strong or skilled she was, to compete with a man in such a sport as football, because unless she was extremely unusual, it would be physically impossible for her to develop the sheer bulk needed for that sport as it is played professionally. Still, there is no reason why women can't compete with other women in football, and in growing numbers of colleges and semipro leagues, they are beginning to do just that—as they already have done in hockey, basketball, and many other traditionally all-male sports. And in sports where physical size is not a factor, such as soccer and baseball, there is no reason why women ultimately could not compete on an equal basis with men—at least no physiological reason.

Getting Strong Mentally

In the first part of this book, I discussed some of the problems that lack of strength can cause women in sports, from less power in hitting a tennis stroke to increased risk of injury. But lack of physical strength is only part of the problem for women athletes. Even if you spend a great deal of time developing your own upper-body strength, you may still not be a winner on the courts. Because of a complex of cultural and psychological pressures, most women, no matter how athletic they may be, tend to settle for a low level of sports achievement.

The major issues of women's rights have become accepted by most of us today: it is assumed that women do deserve equal pay for equal work, for example, and that fathers should share at least some child-rearing responsibilities. But there is still a lingering, pervasive feeling on the part of many women and men that women must defer to men. This attitude has been drilled into us from the time we were young. In my experience and that of my friends—and probably that of most women—it was common to be told repeatedly that "you don't beat boys." If you're good in school, that's fine; but don't be *too* smart, because a boy won't want a girl who is smarter than he is. It's okay to be a good tennis player, but never beat a man at the game—even if you're better than he is. I have a friend, a natural athlete, who taught her boyfriend how to play golf. Even though she had been playing her entire life, he couldn't stand the thought that she always scored lower than he did. One day she confided to me that she occasionally let him win for the sake of his ego. On the other hand, my boyfriend used to let me win occasionally at paddle ball—though he wouldn't admit it. But can you imagine one man letting another win for the sake of his ego? No way! Those boys are out for blood on the fairways, tennis courts, and running tracks. The name of their game is competition, and while, when carried to extremes, it can lead to a lot of ill feelings and ulcers, it can also lead to superior performance in sports. (I am talking here about competition between male peers; of course it's common for a man to let his boss win on occasion—but in this case a different kind of competition is involved.)

Am I saying, then, that women have to become like men in order to win? Of course not, but we do have to learn to develop our competitive side. The lack of a tradition of women's competitiveness is an advantage: we can learn from the mistakes men have made and profit from them, developing a spirit of competition that is just as strong but less selfish than that of men. In the world of marathon running, this new spirit of competition already exists; a woman marathoner of my acquaintance tells of the feeling of sisterhood she always feels when she is running a race. "I want to beat the other woman, sure, and I always run as hard as I can to do it—but at the end of the race we're all proud of each other." In men's marathoning this spirit of camaraderie is often absent. The man wants to beat his archrival, period. And often after the race the loser won't even speak to the winner.

How can you learn to be competitive? For most women, I think the answer lies in learning to believe in yourself. This starts with developing your body and then overcoming fears by going out and playing your sport as well as you can, as often as you can. You can practice hitting tennis balls against a wall ten hours a day for three months in a row, but you're never going to be a good tennis player if you don't go out and play tennis—and play it against better players. One of the side effects of barring girls from playing sports with boys is that, since most girls have not had as much opportunity to develop their sports abilities, the general level of girls' play is lower than that of boys'. As a result, the best girl players never get a chance to play against anyone better.

Because of societal injunctions, it is especially difficult for women to raise their level of play in this manner. In my own experience, I used to be paralyzed on the paddle-ball court with fear at the thought of playing a singles game against one of the street kids. "He'll kill me," was my usual thought. Well, he usually did, but after each such game my own game was a little bit better. My boyfriend, by contrast, actively sought out better players. I remember his triumph when he finally beat a man who had beaten him in every game they had played over a period of three months. But for me, and, I suspect, for most women, once I am beaten by a superior player I tend not to play against him again, because "I'm not good enough." Perhaps I am; perhaps I'm even a better play than he is; but I'm so psyched out over playing against a man that my own game deteriorates.

What's even worse is that I don't generally like to play paddle ball with women I don't know, because with only one exception on my local court, I am embarrassingly better than they are. I'm sure this is because I've been playing mostly with men—and yet I'm not a very good paddle-ball player by anyone's standards.

My friend Fern, who took up squash a year ago, has the same complaint. "I don't really like to play with guys, because they either get nasty when they lose or they hold back and won't really play against me. But I can't find any women who can give me a good game. There are plenty of women at my club who have all the skills, but none of them is really competitive. None of them really wants to win."

And of course the attitude of many male players contributes to women's sense of inferiority in sports. My friend Nan dropped out of a neighborhood volleyball league in disgust. "None of the guys would let me play my position. I mean, the ball could be coming right at me and someone would elbow me out of the way and set it up himself. None of them had any idea whether I could do it myself or not—and they weren't going to take the chance of finding out."

A final psychological factor in our not winning—or not wanting to win—can be summed up by Dr. James A. Peterson. "Most women aren't tough," he says. He means this in two senses: they aren't tough physically, because they haven't trained since they were children; and, just as important, they aren't tough mentally. Most women aren't willing to run that extra mile, lift that heavier weight, jump for that difficult return. We touched on this problem earlier in the book, in the discussion of progressive resistance in weight training. The fact is that success in sports comes with effort, some pain, and a willingness to endure that pain. Competitive men don't even think about this effort and pain; they simply take it for granted. In many cases, of course, it is carried to ridiculous extremes: many male coaches still believe that you're not really working out unless you're in agony. But boys have been exposed to this kind of attitude from the time they were young; they accept it and endure it, however much they hate it; and they become tough and strong as a result of it. Boys who "can't take it" are labeled sissies or girlish. But the boys who *can* take it, even boys who aren't gifted physically, grow up to be much better at sports than most women. They learn to take pain, they learn to work hard, and they learn to hate defeat.

Which is not to say that winning is everything. Of course it isn't. The major joy of most sports is the process, the playing of the sport and the physical release that it brings. But winning, or at least being as good as you can be, is a major part of sports, and you can experience that aspect only by developing your own toughness, physical and mental.

The effects of developing toughness were illustrated dramatically by the experience of the first women's basketball team at West Point. The team was not very good at first, admits Dr. Peterson, their coach. Of the eleven players, three had never played basketball before; to make matters worse, they were unusually short even for a women's team, with one woman only 5'8" and the tallest barely over six feet. In keeping with West Point's policy of treating the new women cadets the same as the men cadets, the Office of Physical Education decided to do just that with the women's basketball team. "This was the first female basketball team that was ever coached just like a men's team," says Peterson. "We expected nothing but the best from our players. Physically, we put them on Nautilus machines to build up their strength. Psychologically, they got their asses kicked when they were bad, and they got rewarded when they did things right."

The results were spectacular. Sunny Jones, a civilian employee in the Office of Information at the Point, describes the team's progress. "At first nobody would come to the games, except as a joke, to look at the freak show. But the women were so fantastic that by half time of the first game everyone in the place was cheering. As the season went on, the word got out, and by the end of the year the gym was so packed that people were sitting three deep along the walls. They weren't coming just to watch women play, either; they were coming to watch good basketball." Sunny tells of a colonel who had fought bitterly to keep women out of West Point and who had only reluctantly been persuaded to attend one of the women's games. "He was sitting right behind me, and by the end of the game he was on his feet yelling, 'Come on, Army!' Not 'Come on, girls,' but 'Come on, Army!'"

The team ended the season with a 15–5 won-lost record, good by anyone's standards. An information officer told me that he felt the turning point in the acceptance of women at the Academy was reached the night of one of the last basketball games, when "one of the women went all out to make an impossible defensive play. She fell into the stands—she could have killed herself—but when she got up she received a standing ovation. No one had realized before that a woman could give a hundred percent just the same as a man."

Largely through the accomplishments of pioneering women athletes like the cadets, stereotypes of women as inferior athletes are beginning to break down. Dr. Stauffer of the Office of Physical Education at West Point feels that girls should be encouraged to play all sports from a young age—and then to stick with their sports through adolescence, which is a time when many "tomboys" drop out of physical activity. According to Dr. Stauffer, there's no real difference in athletic potential between boys and girls up to about age twelve, but "by the tenth grade the girls can't throw or run any longer." Although it is in adolescence that most of the physiological differences between the sexes become evident, Stauffer feels that girls' deterioration in performance is due more to a combination of psychological factors, such as parental pressure on the girls to be "feminine," and boys' unwillingness to continue to play sports with girls, who are obviously maturing more rapidly than they are.

Even women who haven't grown up in an athletic environment can still become very good at most sports (though if you've been sedentary since you were six and you recently took up tennis at age twenty-seven, it's unlikely that you'll ever see Wimbledon). No matter what your background, in fact, Dr. Peterson feels that any deficiencies can readily be overcome. Which is not to say *easily* overcome: it takes work and determination. It takes a willingness to subject yourself to discomfort and to face opponents who are better than you. It takes a willingness to concentrate until you develop a strong desire to win. But along with the psychological toughness necessary for success, your body must be in shape and you must be physically strong.

Even if you don't particularly care about winning or want to develop the toughness that makes a champion, if your body is fit enough for you to play well and easily, you will probably enjoy your game more. So, no matter what your sport and no matter what your level of play, all aspects of your experience in the sport will be enhanced as a result of your getting strong.

Strength and Your Sport

Now that you have finished the Basic Strength Program, you have probably already noticed improvements in some aspects of whatever sports you play. You can probably hit a ball farther, you're faster returning a cross-court shot, you're able to get under the volleyball better. But what about overcoming your own particular weaknesses in the sport? Perhaps you are thinking of taking up a new sport or returning to one you haven't played in years. How can you apply the things you have learned to your performance in specific areas of sports?

In the first part of the book we talked about certain physiological principles relating to exercise. There is a further principle that must be explained here in order to help you decide how best to train for your own sport. That principle is known as the *specificity of exercise*. What this means is that any exercise, whether it involves running, lifting a dumbbell, or even throwing a frisbee, develops strength and coordination primarily for that particular activity. Both swimming and archery develop your back and shoulder muscles (among others), but obviously you would not swim two miles a day just to develop your muscles for archery. While the muscular strength developed by swimming would help your archery game, its main effect would be to improve your ability to swim.

In a 1971 study of Canadian schoolchildren, researchers found that laboratory tests of strength, while important as an overall indicator of fitness, did not correlate with ability to actually perform any given sport. Building strength is an important way to improve your total fitness for sports as well as for daily activity, but it is the *application* of your strength that really counts in sports.

So, when choosing an exercise for a particular sport, you will get the best results if the exercise resembles the movements performed in that sport. An important movement in archery involves drawing the bowstring back; while there are many back-strengthening exercises, an exercise which strengthens your back by drawing your arms back would be better for archery than a back-strengthening exercise which involves bringing your arms up.

In choosing exercises for your own sport, you should continue with the Basic Strength Program (or maintenance program) and add or substitute exercises for each muscle group which are more like the movements in the sport you play.

Bear in mind that how strong you become is ultimately up to you; it depends on the amount of time and effort you want to expend to achieve your sports goals. Most women who continue with the light weights we have been using (whether dumbbells or homemade weights) should experience marked improvement in their own games. If you are a very serious athlete, though, or if you have some other reason to want to become very strong, it will be necessary to move on to a program with heavier weights.

A Note on Heavy Weight Training

It is not within the scope of this book to advise women who plan to train seriously with heavy weights. While most of the principles we have discussed apply to training with weights of any size, once you get beyond the fifteen- or twenty-pound dumbbell phase, you should not continue without supervision, because working with heavy weights incorrectly can be dangerous and cause injury.

Though there are many books on the market describing principles of weight training and suggesting programs, most of them assume that you are already familiar with weight work (which isn't surprising, since most of them are aimed at male athletes). Further, more equipment is necessary for heavy weight training: besides barbells and dumbbells, you need extra plates to attach to them, racks for keeping the equipment, and an exercise bench. For many exercises it is essential to work with a partner who spots you to make sure you don't injure yourself.

For maximum strength gains you must work harder than in our basic program. For best results, you lift what is known as reps maximum (RM), which means a weight that you can lift for a given number of reps (usually eight) until your muscles give out momentarily. It is difficult to find such a weight for all exercises unless you have access to a training machine or a well-equipped gym.

I don't mean to frighten or discourage anyone who is interested in seriously training with weights; in fact, it is my hope that many readers of this book will decide to do just that after having become used to working with weights through the programs in this book. But if you do wish to go beyond the strength gains made through the Basic Strength Program, I urge you to enroll in a weight-lifting course (most Y's offer weight-training courses at a nominal charge in addition to the yearly membership) or to begin your workouts under the supervision of a qualified instructor. Once you have learned how to perform the exercises properly, then, if you have the storage space for equipment, you can continue your workouts at home or can continue without supervision in the gym or Y.

For the majority of women, though, just continuing the basic program and concentrating on the areas which are important for the desired sport should bring dramatic gains in their ability to perform the sport and to enjoy it.

You and Your Sport

The next two chapters show how you can use weight training to improve your own performance. Although many sports are covered, obviously there isn't room for everything; if your own sport isn't listed, think about the basic movements and skills involved in it, and try the exercises suggested for other sports that use similar movements.

In Chapter Twelve are those sports you are most likely to learn in school or in a club (such as archery and softball); in Chapter Thirteen are sports which can be considered "lifetime sports"—sports which you can learn on your own and play your whole life. There will be some overlap, of course: most schools have tennis teams, for example, but I've included tennis with recreational sports because the majority of tennis players do not play in a structured situation.

The Basic Strength Program itself will help you in any sport in a generalized way by developing all of your major muscle groups; although you needn't complete the minimal goals before beginning the exercises suggested for specific sports, you should complete four to six weeks of the Basic Strength Program before you add any new exercises.

Many coaches advocate weight training during the off-season; if yours is a seasonal sport, you should concentrate on building as much strength as possible before the season begins, and then work out less frequently—say once or twice a week—while you are playing.

The suggested exercises for each sport need not be followed rigidly; feel free to substitute other exercises if you wish, but whenever possible try to find exercises that approximate the motion you are trying to develop. Remember also that you may wish to strengthen different areas, depending on the position you play in a sport. Although anyone playing softball will want to work on her throwing ability, an outfielder needs to be able to run quickly, while a catcher may want to strengthen her back and abdominal muscles to a greater extent.

And finally, no matter how much time you devote to getting strong, bear in mind that you will get better at your sport only by playing it—so the final step in any conditioning program for sports is to practice.

12

INDIVIDUAL AND TEAM SPORTS

The following is intended as a guide to help you best develop strength for your own sport. If you are now on a school team or in a sports club, you will get best results by working closely with your coach. Bear in mind that this is only a sampling of individual and team sports. However, many of the exercises are similar in nature, and those that help you in one sport will help you directly in other, similar sports.

Archery

Programs in archery for women are available in all parts of the country, in schools as well as through clubs. As in many sports, women archers are at a disadvantage primarily because of weak upper-body muscles; this is compensated for to a certain extent by use of lighter-weight equipment than that used by men, but it also limits what women can achieve in the sport.

The muscles used in the sport include almost all of the upper-body muscles. To keep the bow steady while you aim, your shoulder muscles come into play; your triceps keeps the bow arm extended; and your biceps and upper-back muscles are used to draw the bowstring.

To improve your skill at archery, then, concentrate on these muscle groups. To your regular exercises for each group in the Basic Strength Program add more weight and increase the number of sets to three each.

For a more specific exercise for the upper back that simulates some of the motions used in archery, add the following supplement to your regular exercise for Group III:

ARM FLING WITH WEIGHTS

Start: Stand comfortably, your arms held straight out in front of you at chest level, a five-pound weight in each hand held in an alternate overhand grip (your palms facing each other).

Move: Pull your arms back, bending your elbows behind you until you feel your shoulder blades touch. Hold three to five seconds, then return to starting position. Repeat. Keep your elbows up and your arms parallel to the floor as you perform this exercise.

Goal: Start with six to eight reps; build to sixteen.

Basketball

The first time an American women's team played a Russian women's team in basketball, the American women were literally overpowered. Quite apart from the fact that the Russian women were generally larger than the Americans, they were far stronger, because they had trained with weights.

As the experience of the women's basketball team at West Point shows, strength training is as important a part of basketball training as the hours spent in front of the hoop learning to aim and sink baskets. If you are now on a school or semipro basketball team, chances are your coach already has you on a strength-building program.

Basketball involves the total body to a greater extent than most sports. Overall strength—upper as well as lower body—and cardiovascular fitness are essential to good performance.

An excellent preliminary exercise for getting in shape for basketball is jogging—at least three or four times a week. Besides improving your cardiovascular fitness, jogging will prepare you for the extensive running required in basketball (pro players run as much as several miles during a game). Because a lot of the running in basketball is in the nature of sprinting, begin to add intervals of sprinting to your jogging program as you improve your fitness. The best way to do this is to add a sprinting workout once a week: jog for a while till you are warmed up, then sprint for thirty seconds (don't run quite as fast as you can, but fast enough to feel the exertion). Follow the sprint with a few more minutes of jogging, then sprint again for thirty seconds. Continue alternating sprinting and jogging. The total amount of sprinting you do will depend on your own level of cardiovascular fitness, but three to five minutes total should greatly improve your ability to run quickly in the kind of stop-and-go way demanded in basketball.

To improve your jumping ability and increase the power of your lower legs, add the calf exercise (I E, p. 94) to your regular exercise for Group I; in addition, increase your reps for the bench step (I B, p. 66). Jumping rope also helps to improve jumping ability, as well as to build leg strength.

Your arms, forearms, and back are important in basketball. One of the most important muscles involved in shooting is the triceps, which straightens your elbow. Add more weight and increase the number of sets to three for your basic triceps exercise (Group

VII), and in addition supplement it with one of the exercises suggested in Chapter Six, the standing press (V F) or the bench press (II F).

For rebounding and general ball handling, upper-back strength is important. Increase the weight used and the number of sets for Group III, and add the supplemental exercise III E, the shoulder shrug (p. 97).

Wrist and hand strength are important in all aspects of the game which have to do with handling the ball. To build your strength in this area, add more weight and reps to your regular exercise for Group VIII, and also add the supplementary exercises VIII E (rubber ball squeeze) and the wrist rotator (see Gymnastics, p. 193).

Diving

Diving is another sport which tends to involve the entire body. Although it would seem that you need mainly leg and hip strength for that jump from the springboard, your trunk muscles are also important to keep your body stabilized as it descends, and your arm and neck muscles help hold your arms locked and your head in position when you enter the water.

Olympic gold-medal diver Micki King used weight training to perfect her own dives, and she advises the girls she coaches to concentrate primarily on leg and abdominal work.

Any of the exercises you have been doing for your legs should help your diving; to improve your jumping power, work on the exercises for jumping suggested in the section on basketball (p. 188).

To improve the strength of your abdominal muscles, do the chair situp (IX B, p. 84) with a weight held under your chin for your regular exercise for this group; in addition, add the supplementary side bend (IX E, p. 104).

To help you hold your arms straight when you enter the water, add more weights and increase the sets to three for your regular exercise for the triceps (Group VII). To further build triceps strength, add as a supplementary exercise for this group either the standing press (II F, p. 100), the bench press (II F, p. 96), or the negative pushup (II C, p. 69).

Finally, neck strength is very important in diving, so you should add the neck exercises (Group X, pp. 105–106) to your regular workout.

Field Hockey

A popular sport for both men and women, field hockey is perhaps the best-known vigorous field team sport widely played by women. It makes demands on the entire body, with special emphasis on overall endurance and leg and arm strength.

Anyone who is serious about hockey should build up her cardiovascular fitness through an aerobic exercise such as running. In addition, add to the amount of weight and increase the sets to three for your regular exercises for the arms and shoulders (Groups V, VI, and VII). Add the arm swing with weights (see Golf, p. 205) to your regular workout for Group V.

Grip strength is important in control of the hockey stick; to improve this aspect of your game, add at least one supplementary exercise to your regular workout for Group VIII.

Finally, field hockey requires leg strength and endurance. To build both, add more reps to your regular exercise for Group I; in addition, particularly if you don't jog, add the knee lift (see Jogging, p. 209), the calf exercise (I E, p. 94), and jump rope.

Football

Football is rapidly becoming available to girls and women in high school and college. If you are now participating in a football program, your coach probably has you on a weight-training program specific to your sport. Many women are beginning to enjoy pickup touch or flag football games in parks and on beaches with other women and men. To become good at the game, no matter what your level of play, you should work on building your overall endurance, the strength of your legs (for running and kicking), and the upperbody muscles used in throwing.

To develop your overall endurance, begin an aerobic exercise such as cycling or running. See also the suggestions for leg strength under Field Hockey, above. The bench step (I B, p. 66) is particularly good for improving your kick.

To improve the strength of your upper body, add more weight and increase the number of sets to three for each exercise in the Basic Strength Program.

The pass in football is similar to the overhand throw in softball; for more specific suggestions on improving your throwing ability, see the section on throwing under Softball (p. 197).

Gymnastics

Since the thrilling performances of Olga Korbut and Nadia Comaneci, gymnastics has captured the hearts and ambitions of young girls all over the world. A friend of mine who teaches this sport feels that anyone can take it up, but urges special caution to men and women over the age of thirty, because of decreased elasticity of tissues and consequently increased chances of joint injury. Many gyms and Y's offer beginning recreational programs in gymnastics for men and women of all ages.

Because gymnastics exercises themselves promote strength (the gymnast's own body provides the resistance), weight training as such is not used as widely in gymnastics as in other sports, except to correct deficiencies of chronically weak muscle groups or to help assure the rapid recovery of an injured muscle.

For women beginning a gymnastics program, the main exercises to emphasize in the Basic Strength Program are those for the upper arms (front and back), the shoulders, and the upper and lower back. Add to your basic program the negative pullup (for Group VI) and the negative pushup (for Group VII).

Flexibility in gymnastics is extremely important for preventing strains and injuries; be sure to spend extra time on your preliminary warmups, particularly if you are just beginning gymnastics.

Neck strength is important in gymnastics, so you should add the neck exercises (Group X, pp. 105–106) to your regular program.

Finally, grip strength is essential in gymnastics. Add more weight and increase the reps for your regular exercise for Group VIII. In addition, add the following supplementary exercise.

WRIST ROTATOR

Start: Stand with feet comfortably apart, arms bent, with your elbows at your side and your forearms straight out in front of you. Hold a weight in each hand in an overhand grip (your palms facing the floor).

Move: Turn both hands until the palms are facing the ceiling, then continue to turn as far as you can. Hold three to five seconds, then slowly turn your hands

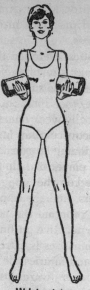

Wrist rotater

back to the starting position and beyond (you are trying to make your palms face out toward the walls).

Goal: Three sets of twelve reps each with a weight of five pounds.

Soccer

It appears that the U.S. has finally caught soccer fever. Long the most popular sport in the world, soccer is starting to appear on playing fields and parks as well as in the curricula of many schools; more important, pro soccer has finally proved that it can attract a mass TV audience as large as that for any other team sport.

Soccer differs from other popular team sports in several significant respects. It does not require equipment other than a soccer ball; it is not violent (although injuries do occur, they are not the sort that are common in such violent contact sports as football and hockey); and, best of all, it is a game that is ideally suited to play by women, because bulk is unimportant. In fact, most world-class soccer players are fairly small men. Agility, a forte of women, is important, as is endurance, which women can readily develop. Furthermore, soccer is a game in which the players act like civilized human beings—it's not at all unusual for one player to help up another player who has been knocked down.

In the Sunday magazine section, the *New York Times* recently speculated that soccer may become the first popular sport in history in which full coed participation will be allowed on all levels: since size is unimportant, there is no reason why we won't someday see coed/professional soccer teams every Sunday afternoon on TV. Indeed, in a 1977 ruling by the New York State Board of Regents, a high school girl was allowed to participate on the boys' varsity team, thus paving the way for future mixed competition.

To prepare for the coming millennium or simply to increase your own enjoyment of soccer, you should improve your cardiovascular fitness, the strength of your legs, and some aspects of your upper-body strength.

The best way to improve your cardiovascular fitness and overall endurance is to begin an aerobic program. Running is an especially good training exercise for soccer, because continual running is a part of the game, and no substitutions are allowed. On a nonprofessional level, the team that can hold out the longest in terms of stamina is often the one that wins.

Running itself will improve the strength of your legs, but to improve your kicking ability, add the exercises suggested for kicking in the section on football (see p. 192). Because of the fast sprints necessary in some phases of the game, add some sprinting intervals to your jogging program. (See Basketball, p. 189.)

Although you don't use your upper-body muscles (except the neck) as much in soccer as in other field sports, you should continue to follow the Basic Strength Program. Add more weight and increase the number of sets to three for your regular exercises for Groups III and V (upper back and shoulders). Also add the shoulder shrug (III E, p. 97) to develop the upper-back muscles, which protect your neck.

Trunk strength, too, is important in soccer: increase the number of reps for both the abdominal exercise (Group IX) and the lower-back exercise (IV).

Finally, since the soccer ball is often played off the head, neck strength is essential. Add the neck exercises (Group X, pp. 105–106) to your regular workout.

Softball

Softball is one of the most widely played of all coed sports. Central Park in New York City is crowded every spring and summer evening with wall-to-wall softball teams playing in various leagues (Restaurants and Bars, Publishing, Advertising, etc.). A rule of most of the leagues is that at least four women must play on each team at all times. In addition to the coed softball boom, pro and semipro all-women softball teams continue in popularity, as do school programs on all levels.

In softball, to a greater extent than in most other team sports, your training will depend on the position you play on the team. To be sure, anyone playing softball must be able to throw and catch, but the requirements of a pitcher are different from those of a fielder.

Whatever your position, though, the most important thing for most women to concentrate on is strength-building exercises to improve throwing and batting skills. The reason men often complain that "girls can't throw" is twofold: first of all, most girls aren't taught the correct way to throw; and secondly—and more important for adults—the muscles involving in throwing are so weak in most women that even correct technique won't help much. Luckily, most of the exercises for throwing will also improve your batting.

For overhand throwing (used by pitchers in men's baseball teams, as well as the fastest and most accurate throw in all fielding maneuvers in softball), the most important muscles involved are those of the shoulders, upper arms, upper back, abdomen, and forearm (for grip).

For underhand throwing, used by the pitcher in slow-pitch softball, the most important muscles are those of the shoulders, the fronts of the upper arms, and the forearms.

To improve your throwing ability, then, increase the amount of weight and increase the sets to three for all your regular exercises for the involved muscle groups.

For both throwing and batting strength, add the following supplementary exercise to your regular exercise for Group V.

SHOULDER ROTATION

Start: Lie on your back, both arms resting on the floor behind you, elbows bent, upper arms out to the sides, forearms at right angles to the upper arms, a weight held in each hand in an overhand grip (your palms facing the ceiling).

Move: Keeping your upper arm and elbow on the floor, lift the weight in your right hand over and down until your hand and the weight are resting on the

Shoulder rotation

floor at about waist level. Your right palm is now facing the floor. At the same time as you return your right hand to starting position, lift your left hand (keeping the upper arm and elbow on the floor) and bring it to the front as you bring the right arm back to starting position. Continue, alternating the direction of your arms. When you perform the rotations, avoid a tendency to let your forearms turn in: keep them at right angles to your upper arms, which remain stretched out to the sides.

Suggested starting weight: Three pounds. Start with two sets of six to eight reps each, build to two sets of twelve reps each, then go on to a heavier weight at six to eight reps.

Goal: Three sets of twelve reps each with a weight of five to eight pounds.

Apart from strengthening the muscles involved in the act of throwing, the most important thing you can do is to throw. Find someone else who wants to improve her softball game, and go out to have a game of catch as many times a week as you can. There is nothing like playing catch for an hour to show you the next day (in sore muscles) how much of your body is involved in the activity of throwing.

Most of the exercises to improve your throwing will also help your batting, as many of the same muscles are involved in both activities. A good supplementary exercise for batting is the bent-over row (III

F); add this to your regular exercise for the upper back.

To stabilize your body while you throw or bat, increase the number of reps for your regular exercise for the lower back (Group IV), as well as for your abdomen (Group IX); add the supplementary side bends (IX E, p. 104).

Grip strength is very important in both batting and throwing. To strengthen your grip, increase the weights and number of reps for your regular exercise for Group VIII. Add as supplementary exercises the rubber ball squeeze (VIII F, p. 103) and the wrist rotator (see Gymnastics, p. 193). This latter exercise will especially help your throwing ability.

Finally, even though endurance isn't as important in softball as in some other sports, a running program will only help your game—both in getting you around the bases, now that you are strong enough to hit a double every time you come up; and on defense, when you have to chase balls out in the field. Because a lot of this running involves fast movement for short distances, include sprinting intervals as described in the section on basketball, p. 189.

Volleyball

Volleyball is considered the most popular and fastest-growing team sport in the U.S. Most women are at a disadvantage when playing volleyball with men because of men's superior jumping and spiking skills, which are, of course, related to men's superior strength.

To improve the strength of your legs for jumping, try the leg exercises suggested for basketball (p. 189). Especially important are the calf exercise (I E) and the bench step (I B). To improve leg strength and endurance, try jumping rope.

The most important upper-body areas to strengthen are your arms and upper back: you need upper-arm strength to block the ball and upper-back strength for spiking and overhead shots. Add to the weight you use and increase the sets to three for your exercises for these groups. In addition, add a supplemental exercise for the triceps (Group VII): the standing press (V F) or bench press (II F).

Finally, your forearms are important in serving and passing. Add more weight and reps to your basic exercise for this group (VIII).

13

RECREATIONAL AND OUTDOOR SPORTS

Bowling

Bowling is one of our oldest known sports; in slightly different form, it was played in medieval times, and today it is one of the most popular participant and spectator sports. Bowling is a sport in which women can compete with men on an equal basis, but a disparity in strength between the sexes, particularly in upper-body strength, can make a real difference in the outcome of the game.

To bowl well, you need strong leg, trunk, arm, and hand muscles.

To increase your leg strength, add more reps to your regular exercise for Group I. In addition, add the supplementary calf exercise (I E, p. 94).

One of the most common problems for women bowlers is an inability to hold the body steady when releasing the ball; to correct this, you should increase the reps for your regular exercise for the lower back (Group IV). In addition, increase the number of situps you are doing in your regular workout, and add the supplementary exercise IX E, side bends (p. 104).

To handle the ball, you need arm and shoulder

strength. Add more weight and increase the number of sets to three for both muscle groups, particularly for Group VII, the backs of the upper arms (triceps). You might also add one of the supplementary exercises for this group, the standing press (V F, p. 100) or the bench press (II F, p. 96).

If you find your hands tiring from the weight of the ball, add supplemental exercise VIII F, the rubber ball squeeze, to your regular exercise for Group VIII.

Cycling

Cycling is a sport which both demands and promotes leg strength and overall endurance. One reason cycling is such an attractive sport is that it can be performed at all levels, from recreational to long-distance touring and serious racing.

The best thing anyone can do to improve her cycling ability is, not surprisingly, to cycle as much as possible. In the winter this can be done on stationary bicycles (available in most gyms and Y's); when the weather is nice, you are limited only by your own fear of traffic and your time schedule.

Jogging is an especially good exercise for women who cycle a lot, because it develops the legs in somewhat different ways, while building cardiovascular fitness. I have a friend, a serious bicycle racer, who tells me that jogging not only improved his endurance for cycling, but helped him get over a recurring knee problem.

Since cycling itself promotes leg strength, you may not wish to do extra strength-building exercises for Group I. If you plan to do long-distance touring, though, add the knee lift (see Jogging, p. 209) and the calf exercise (I E, p. 94) to your regular exercise for Group I. It's also a good idea to perform extra stretching exercises for your legs, such as the calf stretcher and the half-forward bend (see Warmups, p. 61).

You will help to minimize fatigue in long-distance cycling by improving the strength and endurance of your trunk muscles; add more reps to your basic exercises for Groups IV and IX (lower back and abdomen). And always follow a long session on your bike with stretches for the upper body, such as the side stretch (see Warmups, p. 61), shoulder rolls, and arm flings.

Fencing

Although fencing may seem to belong to Douglas Fairbanks movies, it is a popular sport among women all over the country. In my local Y, the enrollment of women in fencing classes is almost as large as that of men. Because of our natural agility, women can become very good fencers, but for superior performance, we need strength in our legs, shoulders, and arms, and particularly in the hands, wrists, and forearms.

To improve your own fencing, add to the amount of weight and increase your sets to three for each of the muscle groups named above in your Basic Strength Program.

Because grip strength is so important, add the following two supplementary exercises to your regular exercise for Group VIII: the rubber ball squeeze (VIII F, p. 103) and the wrist rotator (see Gymnastics, p. 193).

Frisbee

Although some people do not consider frisbee a true sport, there is no question that it is one of the most popular outdoor recreational pursuits in America, with local tournaments and even national championships. Since the equipment is eminently portable, frisbee is played everywhere, from the streets and parks to country fields and beaches.

A great deal of strength isn't as important in frisbee as in some other activities, but increasing your upper-body strength should improve your coordination and accuracy. The most important muscles used in frisbee-throwing are those of the upper-back, upper-arm, wrist, and abdomen.

If you are seriously into frisbee, add the following exercises to your basic program: the shoulder shrug (III E, p. 97) and the side bends (IX E, p. 104). In addition, increase the amount of weight and reps for your forearm exercise (Group VIII), and add the supplementary wrist rotator (see Gymnastics, p. 193).

Golf

Golf's popularity is undoubtedly due to the fact that not only is it a challenging game, but it provides an excuse to spend a nice day out of doors. Since it's not too strenuous, golf can also be quite companionable for players who aren't out for blood. Golf is a good sport for women, and one that has been played by both sexes for many years: it is reported that Mary Queen of Scots, among other royal ladies, was an avid golfer.

I will never forget the two summers a number of years ago when I tried to learn how to play golf. In spite of my many hours on the course and practicing at the driving range, I couldn't manage to hit the ball more than a few yards—and never in a straight line. I finally gave up the whole attempt in disgust. Alas, if I had only known then that poor upper-body strength was a major cause of my ineptitude, I might be out on the fairways today.

Although some degree of leg strength is necessary for golf, the most important muscles involved are those of the arm and upper back. For stability, the trunk muscles should also be strong, particularly the side abdominal muscles.

To improve your golf game, add more weight and increase the sets to three in your basic program for the shoulders (Group V) and the triceps (Group VII); these muscles are important in the swing, especially the triceps, which keeps your arm straight. In addition, add the following exercise as a supplement to your regular exercise for Muscle Group III (upper back):

ARM SWING WITH WEIGHTS

Start: Stand comfortably, feet apart, arms at your sides, holding weights in each hand in an overgrip (your palms are facing behind you).

Move: Keeping your body straight, raise the weights behind you as far as you can; lower to start, then lift them in front of you as far as you can. Return to start and repeat the entire sequence, slowly and rhythmically.

Suggested starting weight: Three pounds. Start with two sets of six to eight reps each, build to two sets of twelve, then move on to two sets of six to eight reps each.

Goal: Three sets of twelve reps each with a weight of eight to ten pounds in each hand.

Comment: The effect of this exercise is a continuous swing, but be careful not to let gravity take over the work of lowering the weight on either of the downward parts of the exercise; instead, lower the weights

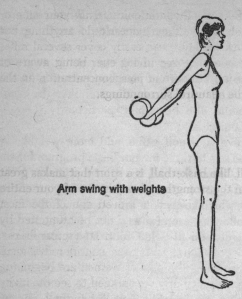

Arm swing with weights

with a controlled motion. Remember to keep your head still throughout the exercise (as you would while actually swinging a golf club).

To improve the range of motion for your hips and shoulders in the golf swing, place a golf club over your shoulders and hold on to it with both hands while you twist and turn your torso as far as you can, first in one direction and then the other.

For trunk stability, add the side bends (IX E, p. 104) to your regular exercise for Muscle Group IX (abdomen).

Extremely important to the game of golf are the muscles of your forearms, wrists, and hands. To strengthen these, add one or more supplementary exercises to your basic forearm exercise (Group VIII). Especially good are the rubber ball squeeze (VIII F, p. 103) and the wrist rotator (see Gymnastics, p. 193).

Finally, for overall conditioning, *walk* your nine or eighteen holes. A golf cart doesn't do anything but burn precious fuel. You can easily cover several miles in an afternoon of golf without ever being aware of all that walking, because of your concentration on the game and the beautiful surroundings.

Handball

Handball, like basketball, is a sport that makes great demands on the strength and endurance of your entire body. Four-wall handball is indeed one of the most vigorous of all sports, and should not be attempted by anyone who does not have good cardiovascular fitness. Although handball has long been considered a men-only sport, growing numbers of women are beginning to play it. I'm particularly encouraged to see the many teenaged girls who play one-wall handball on my neighborhood schoolyard handball courts.

Because endurance and cardiovascular fitness are so important in handball, this is a sport in which aerobic conditioning is a must: to achieve this, you should jog, cycle, or swim at least three times a week.

Virtually all of your muscles are involved in handball. To improve your throwing ability, add the supplementary exercises for the upper body suggested in the section on softball (p. 197), and add one or more supplemental exercises for your forearm (Group VIII), especially the wrist rotator (p. 193) and the rubber ball squeeze (VIII F, p. 103).

To improve your agility and trunk stability, add more reps to your basic exercises for the lower back (Group IV) and the abdomen (Group IX); also add the side bends (IX E) to your regular abdominal exercise.

Hiking

As more women take to the trails, backpacking, hiking, and even rock climbing, more of us are realizing how poorly conditioned we are for these activities. The two most important areas of fitness for any activity involving a lot of walking and climbing are leg strength and overall endurance.

The best and fastest way for you to improve both of these aspects of your fitness is to begin an aerobic program; because you want to emphasize leg strength, jogging or cycling would be best. In addition, add the knee lift (see Jogging, p. 209) and calf exercise (Supplemental Exercise I E, p. 94) to your regular exercise for Muscle Group I. If you expect to do a lot of climbing, also include a few minutes of the bench step (I B, p. 66).

Women who carry packs will also want to improve all aspects of their upper-body strength and endurance, particularly the shoulders, upper back, and trunk muscles (abdomen and lower back). Increase the amount of weight and sets and/or reps for each of these muscle groups when you perform your regular exercises.

Jogging (Running)

Jogging can be all things to all people: an aerobic conditioning exercise for those who want to get in shape, a pleasant and relaxing pastime, and a serious way of training for long-distance races. Jogging is probably the ideal sport for women, because it can be performed almost anywhere, it can be done alone or with other people, and it requires no skill or previous athletic training. The main muscles used in jogging are the leg muscles and, to a lesser extent, the lower-back and abdominal muscles.

There is no need to add any exercises to the Basic Strength Program if you are just beginning to jog; the best way to build your strength and endurance is to start with a gradual walk-jog program (see the Selected Bibliography for books on aerobic conditioning programs). But after you have been jogging for a few months, or if you want to develop your speed for racing, you should add the following exercises to your regular workout for Muscle Group I. Since jogging develops the back leg muscles relatively more than the front leg muscles, these exercises will help you maintain a balance between muscle groups; also, they may help to prevent some jogging-related injuries.

KNEE LIFT

Start: Sit on a table that is high enough to let your legs dangle down without touching the floor. Hang a weight over the toes of one foot. The easiest way to do this is to fill an empty paint bucket with enough sand to make it weigh three to five pounds; then just hang the handle, wrapped in a towel, over your foot.

Move: Slowly, keeping your leg straight, lift your lower leg, from the knee. Hold for three to five seconds, then slowly lower. Repeat, then perform the exercise with the other leg.

Goal: Start with twelve reps; build to twenty-five with each leg.

ANKLE LIFT

Start: Sit on a table as for the knee lift, with a weight of three to five pounds hanging from the toes of one foot.

Move: This time, bend your foot up at the ankle, lifting the weight as you do so. Hold for three to five seconds, then lower. Repeat, then switch legs.

Goal: Start with twelve reps; build to twenty-five with each foot.

It is a good idea for joggers, particularly those who run more than five or six miles a week, to do extra situps for abdominal strength. This is because jogging develops the lower back relatively more than the abdomen, and if this imbalance becomes too great, it can result in postural problems, pain, and even injury.

Finally, warming up is as important for jogging as for the Basic Strength Program. The stretching warm-ups suggested in Chapter Five (pp. 61–63) are all good as preliminaries to your daily jog.

Racket Sports

Although it is obvious that the various racket sports are different in many ways, in others they are similar enough that a strength-building program for tennis will be helpful for squash, paddle ball, paddle and platform tennis, racquet ball, and even badminton (which historically is not even related to these other sports). For that reason, I am lumping the racket sports together, although you will probably want to modify the suggestions here, depending on your own game and needs. Badminton, for example, does not require quite so much strength as tennis, while squash is one of the most vigorous of all sports and requires a very high degree of cardiovascular fitness and over-all endurance.

Tennis is a sport which has long been considered respectable for women. As with many other sports, it is primarily lack of upper-body strength that causes problems for women players: our natural agility makes tennis a good game for us, but upper-body weakness limits the power and speed of our service and returns. Although strength training for women in tennis was almost unheard of even three years ago, today growing numbers of women on the pro circuit are training with weights: these include Margaret Court and Julie Anthony, both of whom credit weight training with having improved the strength of their serve.

To improve your own service, as well as your other shots, you must improve your arm, shoulder, and grip strength. Increase the amount of weight you use and increase the number of sets to three for each of these muscle groups. In addition, add the arm swing with weights (see Golf, p. 205) to your regular exercise for Group V (shoulders).

Don't forget the importance of your forearm and grip strength: add more weight and increase the number of sets for your basic exercise for Group VIII, and add as supplements the rubber ball squeeze (VIII F, p. 103) and the wrist rotator (see Gymnastics, p. 193).

Especially important in the backhand are your forearms, triceps, and upper back. If your backhand is weak, you will want to concentrate on these muscle groups particularly by adding more weight, sets, and supplementary exercises.

The trunk muscles, too, are important in tennis. Try adding more reps to your regular exercise for the lower back (Group IV), and add the side bend (IX E, p. 104) to your regular abdominal exercise.

Finally, because tennis requires stamina if you plan to play several sets, an aerobic conditioning program is advisable: jogging would be best, because it will also strengthen your leg muscles. To help you move quickly around the court, add intervals of sprints to your jogging as you become more conditioned (see Basketball, p. 189).

Rowing (Including Canoeing)

Joan Lind, the champion Olympic rower, was once quoted in *WomenSports* as saying, "There isn't a decent woman rower in the world who doesn't treat weight training seriously." Although this may seem an extreme statement, it isn't, given most women's poor upper-body strength. For whether you are interested in competition or just going out on the lake on a Sunday afternoon, two essentials for effective rowing are torso and arm strength.

To develop torso strength, increase the reps for your regular exercise for Group IV (lower back) and Group IX (abdomen). In addition, add IX E, the side bend, p. 104, to your regular exercise for Group IX.

To increase the endurance and strength of your arms, add more weight and increase the number of sets to three for your regular exercises for Group VI (biceps) and Group VII (triceps). If you have access to a chinning bar, negative chinups (VI F, p. 101) should be added to your regular workout for this group.

Upper-back strength is extremely important in the action of rowing. To your regular exercise for this muscle group, add the arm fling with weights (see Archery, p. 188) and supplemental exercise III F, the bent-over row.

Because your hands may tire easily when rowing for a long time, increase the number of reps of your regular exercise for Group VIII.

And finally, if you belong to a gym or Y, work out often on a rowing machine, which will develop the muscles used in your sport in a direct and efficient way.

Skating

Ice skating is a favorite pastime all over the country; in areas where it doesn't freeze, you can usually find one or more commercial indoor ice rinks. Roller skating, while not possessing quite the popularity of ice skating, remains a popular recreation in many areas (although apparently among children it is being replaced by skateboarding).

As anyone who has tried to skate—particularly to ice skate—for the first time knows, a great deal of leg and ankle strength is required. In addition, endurance is important, especially if you are planning to skate for any length of time.

The ideal exercise both to strengthen your legs and to build your endurance is jogging. If you are very serious about skating, add supplemental exercises for the leg to your basic exercise for Group I. Especially helpful would be the calf exercise (I E, p. 94), the knee lift, and the ankle lift (see Jogging, p. 209).

Upper-body strength, particularly torso strength, is important for figure skating. Add the side bends (IX E) to your regular abdominal exercise, and increase the number of reps of your regular exercise for Group IV, the lower back.

Skiing

Skiing is rapidly becoming one of the most popular sports in the country: in its three forms, alpine skiing, water skiing, and cross-country skiing, it manages to appeal to just about everybody. Skiing is a sport at which women can excel and in which they are accepted on all levels, from recreational to competitive. Further, skiing is an especially good coed sport, one in which athletes of varying abilities can participate together.

All three types of skiing emphasize endurance, leg strength, and upper-body strength. In addition to doing the Basic Strength Program, you should add supplementary exercises for Group I, the legs. The bench step (I B, p. 66) and the calf exercise (I E, p. 94) should be added to your basic program before the skiing season begins. The knee lift and ankle lift (see Jogging, p. 209) will further help to condition your legs.

For body stability, increase your reps for Group IX (abdomen), and add the side bends (with weights) (IX E, p. 104). Add more reps to your regular exercise for Group IV (lower back).

For poling, upper-back, shoulder, and arm strength are important; in each of these groups, increase the amount of weight and the number of sets to three in your regular workout.

Endurance and cardiovascular fitness are especially important for cross-country skiing; in the off-season it's important to maintain a vigorous aerobic program such as jogging. Since cross-country skiing itself is the most vigorous of all aerobic sports, it is an excellent activity to take up for overall conditioning. It is far less expensive than alpine skiing and can be done in parks, on golf courses, or in almost any clear area where there is an accumulation of snow.

Swimming

Swimming, like jogging, is one of the best sports for women, because it is an aerobic exercise and an excellent overall body conditioner. Swimming involves virtually all of your muscles, and while it will tend to strengthen them, your own swimming will be improved as a result of your building upper-body strength.

Particularly important in swimming are your arm, shoulder, chest, and upper-back muscles. To improve the strength of your upper back and the backs of your shoulders, add the bent-over row (III F) as a supplement for Group III, and the arm swing with weights (see Golf, p. 205) to your regular exercise for Group V (shoulders). For all exercises, increase your reps (for endurance) and increase the number of sets to three.

Trunk strength, too, is important in swimming; add more reps to your regular exercise for the lower back (Group IV), and supplement your regular abdominal exercise (Group IX) with the side bends (IX E).

14

STAYING STRONG THROUGH LIFETIME SPORTS

A few years ago, when I was married, sedentary, and working at an incredibly high-pressure job, my husband once said of me, "She works like an animal." To give you an idea of my state of mind at that time, I took his remark as a compliment. It was not until I began jogging and working out that I realized that all work and no play was making me not only a dull person but an unhealthy and unhappy one as well. I came to realize that the statement itself contained a fallacy: even an animal knows when to take a little time out to relax and play. If you doubt this, watch your dog or cat out in the yard chasing butterflies or just lying around observing the passing scene. In the wild, too, animals will spontaneously stop their work of gathering food, building nests, or hunting and take a snooze or engage in some play.

We are animals, too, and each of us needs that time out to relax, to unwind through play. Although the competitive aspect is important, ultimately this is the basic value of all sports: the play, the enjoyment of doing it. Part of that enjoyment, of course, comes in learning to perfect your backhand, to hit home runs, to break the eight-minute mile. But another very important part is the relaxation and fun of it, which should never be lost even at the highest levels of competition. It may seem strange to think of exertion as relaxing, but anyone who works out or plays a sport regularly knows that the fatigue at the end of a few sets of tennis or a long swim is exhilarating, a sign that your body is being active and is renewing itself in the process.

Once you are fit, you will find that you can continue to play sports throughout your life. One reason there are so few elderly people participating in vigorous sports is that most of these people have long since lost the conditioning that would enable them to play these sports without undue fatigue or injury. (Of course, your reaction time and coordination deteriorate as you get older, but there are different levels of play for all sports.) Furthermore, as you continue to play sports you will find that the sport itself will help you to maintain your level of conditioning.

How do you decide what sports to play? The best answer is to choose those you enjoy (and have access to). If you have the time for only one sport, then of course that sport should be aerobic: swimming, cycling, jogging, cross-country skiing. But there is no need to stop at one sport: many people (like me) enjoy learning new skills and developing new interests throughout their lives. Any of the sports mentioned in the last chapter can be played as a lifetime sport.

No sport by itself will be enough to maintain total fitness, but it is easy to choose sports that emphasize different aspects of fitness, and to fit them in with your regular workouts. Besides the aerobic sports mentioned above, other sports which tend to improve cardiovascular fitness include canoeing, backpacking, and mountain climbing. Sports which particularly emphasize strength are gymnastics, judo, karate, and rowing.

Another thing to keep in mind is that your basic build helps determine the activities you are most suited for. To put it another way, each woman is simply built better for some sports than for others.

For example, if you are tall and skinny and have long, fragile limbs, your best sport is most likely one which does not require bulk or a great deal of strength, such as distance running. A woman with a constant weight problem will find it more difficult to perform activities requiring much strength or agility, but she should be good at swimming, because of her greater buoyancy; a woman who is naturally muscular and heavy-boned will probably tend to be good at most sports she tries.

This is not to say that it is impossible for a skinny woman to be good at wrestling or for an overweight woman to play tennis well; many other physical factors, such as the length of your bones and the efficiency of your nervous system, help to determine athletic success. Furthermore, such psychological factors as motivation and concentration may be the ultimate determinants of success in any field.

Having a realistic picture of your physical limitations as well as your strengths can help you to choose the activities you will be best at as well as those you will most enjoy. If you have a lifelong weight problem, you should probably forget about marathoning, at least at the championship level, but less vigorous activities, such as golf or recreational cycling, combined with a good diet will help you keep your weight under control as well as giving you physical pleasure. If you are a natural klutz who is always tripping over cracks in the sidewalk and spraining her ankle, you will probably have to devote more time than other women athletes both to improving your strength (strong ankles are less likely to get sprained) and to practicing the skills in any sport.

Whatever sport or sports you choose, remember that the best way to get good at that sport is to practice and play it as often as you can. If you are now in school, you have a rare opportunity to discover new sports. Go out for teams whenever you can. Don't let the idea that you're not good enough scare you— the only way to get good is to play the sport.

Similarly, if you are long out of school, there is no reason to deny yourself the fun of any sport that attracts you, once you are strong and fit. Most Y's and many adult education courses offer instruction in the basic skills of a wide variety of sports. There is room in the world of sport for all types of personality and all levels of ability—and there are enough different activities to accommodate everyone. Even physically handicapped athletes are learning to play softball, to run races, to bowl.

Because of increased leisure time and new opportunities for women in all areas of life, I believe we are entering a golden age for women in sports. For too many years, women have been spectators; now is our chance to be doers, to be athletes. Now is our chance to discover something which many men have long known—the beauty, power, and physical pleasure of using our bodies with precision and strength, of setting out to achieve something physically and accomplishing it, of being aware of the feel of muscles being stretched, joints moving, the whole body and mind working as a unit. Finally, whatever the level of play, it's our chance to discover the essential *joy* of sport: the thrill of hitting a golf ball high and straight; the excitement of solidly returning a serve to the far corner of the opposite court; the exhilaration of running alongside a river, your own breathing the loudest sound in nature, the rhythmic fall of your steps and swing of your arms so automatic that you are unaware of any effort, only of the natural pleasure and beauty of your body in motion.

AFTERWORD

Perhaps the most striking result of the societal upheavals produced by the women's liberation movement is that at last women have choices: the choice to marry or stay single, to be mothers or not, to stay at home or to work—in short, to determine the direction of our own lives. And finally, we are achieving choice in what may be the most important area of all: the choice to liberate our bodies. No longer need women sit back and watch men play sports; no longer must we be weak and helpless and dependent; no longer must women resign themselves to progressive flabbiness, decay, and physical obsolescence past the age of twenty-five.

In recent years I have had occasion to meet an increasing number of successful, creative women who are also athletes. These include my friend Fern, a runner and squash player who manages a busy housewares department in a large New York store; Nina Kuscsik, who at age thirty-eight is a nurse, mother of three, and world-class marathoner; and a busy editor I know who has been working out with weights for four years and plays almost every sport you can mention. What these women all have in common is that they are successful in their professional and personal lives, and they are physically active.

I have a theory that realizing one's potential proceeds along the lines of a file of standing dominos: if you tip one domino on the end, the rest inevitably fall. I believe that something like this happens when anyone sets out to improve herself physically. One beneficial change directly and inevitably leads to another physical development, leading to even more physical development, as well as to mental and emotional development.

In my own case, the first domino stood until I was nearly thirty years old. At that time I was helpless, or believed myself to be, in nearly all areas of my life. I was a sedentary, overweight slave to cigarettes, fearful and nervous, dependent on those around me, and barely on speaking terms with my body. Then I began a running program, and the first domino fell. As I continued to run I discovered that even I, possibly the most unathletic person who ever lived, had a body capable of physical improvement and enjoyment. The self-confidence this discovery gave me enabled me to branch out physically, to take up a sport for the first time in my life and become good at it, to want to become strong, to further improve and integrate my body into my life. After the first flush of this new physical self-confidence, the dominos began rapidly falling in areas other than the physical: confidence in my body gave me mental and emotional confidence, and I began to venture into new avenues in my career. Getting strong itself has started a new line of falling dominos; lately I'm looking forward to taking up cross-country skiing and the martial arts; and, most important, I have the confidence to know that I will be able to do them, even if not at a championship level.

Any woman can improve herself in any area of her life. And once you have made one change, you will find that other changes flow naturally and inevitably. Whether it is for sports, for the improvement of your figure, or simply for the well-being that good health brings, by developing your physical potential you are also developing your potential in all other areas: mental, emotional, and even spiritual. The ancient Greeks believed in the ideal of "a sound mind in a sound body." For myself, at least, and I believe for most women, the one cannot exist without the other, and the two reinforce each other in every way.

SELECTED BIBLIOGRAPHY

BOOKS ON AEROBICS AND RUNNING

Aerobics for Women, by Mildred and Kenneth H. Cooper, Bantam, 1972, $1.50.

This book, based on the earlier *Aerobics,* and *New Aerobics,* fully explains the theory of aerobic conditioning. Especially valuable are the charts that give graduated programs in all aerobic exercises and allow easy comparison among the different types of aerobic exercises.

The Complete Book of Running, by James F. Fixx, Random House, 1977, $10.00.

This well-written and entertaining book tells you everything you need to know about running, based on the author's own experiences and on interviews with hundreds of runners and experts.

The Runner's Handbook: A Complete Guide for Men and Women on the Run, by Robert Glover and Jack Shepherd, Viking, 1978.

Just what the title promises. Aimed more toward the competitive runner than the beginner, although beginning programs are included.

Running for Health and Beauty: A Complete Guide for Women, by Kathryn Lance, Bobbs-Merrill, 1977, $4.95 (paper), $8.95 (hardcover).

A basic guide for women who have never run before.

Women's Running, by Dr. Joan Ullyot, World Publications, 1976, $3.95.

A guide for women who are interested in running competitively.

BOOKS ON GENERAL PHYSICAL FITNESS

The West Point Fitness and Diet Book, by Colonel James L. Anderson and Martin Cohen, Rawson Associates, 1977, $10.95.

A very thorough book on all aspects of physical fitness, from strength to aerobic conditioning to diet. There are special sections and programs for people of all ages, and a well-illustrated section on training with light weights.

The Official YMCA Physical Fitness Handbook, by Clayton R. Myers, Popular Library, 1975, $1.50.

This book gives a wide variety of exercises for muscular and skeletal conditioning and advocates a comprehensive approach to fitness.

BOOKS ON WEIGHT TRAINING

Most popular books on weight training are aimed at men who are interested in competitive weight lifting or body building. The following two books are more accessible to women than most:

Complete Weight Training Book, by Bill Reynolds, World Publications, 1977, $6.95.

This easy-to-read and informative book tells you everything you need to know about weight training with light and heavier weights, and includes many strength-building programs for sports as well as for general conditioning.

Strength Training by the Experts, edited by Daniel P. Riley, Leisure Press, 1977.

This book is a collection of articles. In addition to weight-training exercises with free-standing weights and weight-training machines, the book provides detailed information on the physiology of strength training.

INDEX

ABOUT THE AUTHOR

KATHRYN LANCE, photographed on the cover, was born in El Paso and lives in New York City, where she has been running ten miles a week for nearly five years. She has written *Running For Health and Beauty: A Complete Guide For Women,* as well as numerous articles, stories and education guides for educational journals and textbooks, and for three years wrote for the soap operas *All My Children* and *One Life to Live.*

How's Your Health?

Bantam publishes a line of informative books, written by top experts to help you toward a healthier and happier life.

☐	10350	**DR. ATKINS' SUPERENERGY DIET,** Robert Atkins, M.D.	$2.25
☐	12719	**FASTING: The Ultimate Diet,** Allan Cott, M.D.	$1.95
☐	12762	**WEIGHT CONTROL THROUGH YOGA** Richard Hittleman	$1.95
☐	11872	**A DICTIONARY OF SYMPTOMS,** Gomez	$2.25
☐	6417	**THE BRAND NAME NUTRITION COUNTER,** Jean Carper	$1.95
☐	12607	**SWEET AND DANGEROUS,** John Yudkin, M.D.	$2.25
☐	12362	**NUTRITION AGAINST DISEASE,** Roger J. Williams	$2.25
☐	12174	**NUTRITION AND YOUR MIND,** George Watson	$2.25
☐	12360	**THE NEW AEROBICS,** Kenneth Cooper, M.D.	$2.25
☐	12468	**AEROBICS FOR WOMEN,** Kenneth Cooper, M.D.	$2.25
☐	12737	**THE ALL-IN-ONE CARBOHYDRATE GRAM COUNTER,** Jean Carper	$1.95
☐	12415	**WHICH VITAMINS DO YOU NEED?** Martin Ebon	$2.25
☐	12107	**WHOLE EARTH COOKBOOK,** Cadwallader and Ohr	$1.95
☐	10865	**FASTING AS A WAY OF LIFE,** Allan Cott, M.D.	$1.75
☐	12718	**THE ALL-IN-ONE CALORIE COUNTER,** Jean Carper	$1.95
☐	11402	**THE FAMILY GUIDE TO BETTER FOOD AND BETTER HEALTH,** Ron Deutsch	$2.25

Buy them at your local bookstores or use this handy coupon for ordering:

Bantam Books, Inc., Dept. HN, 414 East Gulf Road, Des Plaines, Ill. 60016

Please send me the books I have checked above. I am enclosing $_____ (please add 75¢ to cover postage and handling). Send check or money order —no cash or C.O.D.'s please.

Mr/Mrs/Miss_____

Address_____

City_____State/Zip_____

HN—2/79

Please allow four weeks for delivery. This offer expires 8/79.

Bantam Book Catalog

Here's your up-to-the-minute listing of over 1,400 titles by your favorite authors.

This illustrated, large format catalog gives a description of each title. For your convenience, it is divided into categories in fiction and non-fiction—gothics, science fiction, westerns, mysteries, cookbooks, mysticism and occult, biographies, history, family living, health, psychology, art.

So don't delay—take advantage of this special opportunity to increase your reading pleasure.

Just send us your name and address and 50¢ (to help defray postage and handling costs).